GRIEF

A Path of Loss and Light

Swamini Sri Lalitambika Devi

MAHAKAILASA ASHRAM
NEW YORK, NEW YORK

ISBN 978-0-9778633-6-5

For the Nectar Jewel.
You are always my Mother.

TABLE OF CONTENTS

PREFACE

I am young on the path of renunciation. I do not claim to be fully awakened. I face the same emotional challenges that anyone else might. I cannot say that I have transcended the mind or merged with the absolute, such that I am completely dispassionate, even as there are glimpses of truth.

Last year, I cared for a loved one who was dying. He was innocent, joyful, loving, and completely surrendered to this situation that neither of us could change—his dying.

I kept a journal during this time. It helped to balance the mind, so that I could continue to care for him with wisdom, compassion, and strength. I loved him. Though he lived at the temple for only nine months, his death was an incredible loss. I mourn him deeply.

Students have commented that teachers don't talk enough about how they grieve. Perhaps none of us talks enough about how much we love, either.

It is important also to realize that teachers are students, and students are teachers. In fact, we can bow down to everyone we meet along this path to liberation as our teacher.

As a simple seeker who prays to merge with the light, I offer this book, based on a journal of grief and renewal, at your feet.

There is no one who will not lose a loved one, even as we will all realize the ultimate truth of light and salvation. Speaking honestly about our shared experiences is a way to support each other along the path to awakening.

Detachment may be one of many monastic, or simply spiritual, ideals. Indeed we learn not to be carried away by our passions. We mature emotionally, like slowly ripening fruit. We seek inner peace, the truth of the Lord, so that we can serve with kind equanimity and without expectation.

When emotion does arise, however, we stay connected to the feelings.

In being attentive to emotion, our wounds heal. So, the fear, anger, sorrow, and insecurity melt away in the sunrise of unconditional love.

The great souls express this truth of love in the way they live their lives.

Consider the example of Jesus Christ.

Christ was an incarnation, the Son of the Father. His teachings have changed the world for us all.

In the Sermon on the Mount, he gives us the eight Beatitudes as a path to follow.

To meditate upon these is to follow in the footsteps of Jesus.

Blessed are the poor in spirit,
for they shall inherit the earth.

Blessed are those who mourn,
for they shall be comforted.

Blessed are the meek,
for they shall inherit the earth.

Blessed are those who hunger
and thirst for righteousness,
for they shall be filled.

Blessed are the merciful,
for they shall be shown mercy.

Blessed are the pure in heart,
for they shall see God.

Blessed are the peacemakers,
for they shall be called children of God.

11

Blessed are those who are persecuted
for righteousness' sake,
for theirs is the kingdom of heaven.

Matthew 5:3-12

Jesus was a true teacher.

He was also a divine presence who healed the sick and raised the dead.

Even so, he experienced human emotion.

Jesus expressed anger when he overturned the tables in a temple which he felt had been made into a marketplace.

Jesus felt fear in the Garden of Gethsemane, when his sweat was as drops of blood. He prayed that the Father might take this cup of the Crucifixion from him, even as he surrendered to the Father's will.

Jesus grew tired, fell, and needed help in carrying the cross to Mount Calvary.

Jesus knew sorrow and abandonment during the Crucifixion, when he cried out, "Father, Father, why have you forsaken me?"

Jesus was also a presence of true love. He asks us to be so, too.

A new commandment I give to you—
to love one another.
As I have loved you,
so you should love one another.   John 13:34

Jesus was the word of the Lord, embodied. Like the Crucifix itself, he is an intersection, a crossroads between the earth below and heavens above. He was of both flesh and Spirit, as are we.

Opening to ourselves as human beings with rich emotional lives allows us to awaken. In feeling our joys and sorrows with an equal heart, we are able to be fully present for the glory, as well.

—*Swamini Sri Lalitambika Devi*

Grief is full
of the longing
that leads straight
to truth.

To one who knows truth
without a word
being spoken,
there is no longer
grief
in longing.

The heart splits
wide
with laughter
at the slightest touch.

To one who lives silent
as the sweet hibiscus
burnt to ash
in the fire
of devotion,
grief is laughter,
grief is laughter.

PART I

JANUARY 18-MARCH 16, 2010

January 18, 2010

7:39p.m.

The Son is dying.

If the Mother can't get the needle in to give him the treatment, he's going to die.

Even if the Mother can get the needle in, he's going to die. And he hates it. He tenses up and winces when the Mother tries, because she's not very good at it.

He lies here now, languid on the couch.

The needles face him in a small cardboard box, beside stacked prayer books, on a bookshelf.

The Mother tries to give him the treatment in the morning and again in the evening.

12:33a.m.

The Mother is not sure that this treatment is helpful.

Over the weekend, she finally got the needle in and gave the Son a full dose of fluids.

He barely ate for three days.

Earlier today, he was supposed to receive the fluids, again.

The Mother couldn't do it, and he has eaten almost a full lunch.

Now, the dishes are cleaned and dried.

She sifts through the mail. She notes bill after bill, along with several notices for low-interest rate credit cards.

Why do people so rarely send personal cards, anymore?

"Don't Know." She sees this written on the postcard she has received from a local Zen center that she visited once. This kind of mind is supposed to be liberated. Don't Know Mind.

Today, "I don't know," doesn't seem like such a good thing.

What should I do?

Any doctor they visit will say, "Give him the treatment." *So, why does the treatment seem to make him sicker? Would there be less suffering for both of us, just to let him be?*

The Mother contemplates these questions as she sits and watches him sleep.

He is thin and freckled, with a striped blanket pulled up to his chin.

Life—It's a terminal condition. We're all going to die. Watching this happen to someone we love is difficult.

He smiles peacefully in his sleep.

The Son is innocent and gentle. He doesn't deserve this, but then, who deserves it?

…don't know.

January 19, 2010

9:42a.m.

This morning, the Mother is surprised that the Son still loves her, that he still wants her to hold him.

She did, after all, spend much of yesterday piercing him with needles.

Her hair veils her face, as she leans over to stroke his cheek.

1:30p.m.

The Mother leaves the Son only briefly to meet with a meditation student. The two sit across from each other on futons that they have pulled close. The student is a recovering alcoholic.

She is currently working the fourth step— taking inventory.

"Resentment may be the root of suffering. This is why we take inventory," she says.

Whom do I feel resentful towards? Why? What behaviors in this person are bringing up these feelings in me? We ask ourselves these questions.

22

And then, *What is my Achilles heel? What is the weakness in me that causes me to react so strongly.*

This is where the work begins, within.

We don't point the accusatory finger or lay insistent blame. We calmly investigate our own reactions.

The Mother considers the nature of relationship.

There is a particular chemistry between people. Person X will react differently to Person Y than to Person Z.

Perhaps, none of this is personal. It's just chemistry that yields a puff of smoke, a small explosion, or a new and fantastic compound.

So we relate with circumstance, too.

Reaction simply means that there is work to be done.

The Mother notes her reactions to the Son's illness. In witnessing these reactions, in seeing through the smokescreen of emotion, she will be better able to care for him.

4:17p.m.

This afternoon, the Mother is working at the streamlined laptop computer, when the

Son lays his hand on hers and asks her quietly to stop.

"Don't work," he says. "I'm dying."

Perhaps she should leave work aside, to be with him. This may be the right thing to do—to forget about "responsibilities," to let the world be what it is, to disappear, as if into cloud-covered mountains, to receive the gift of this time together.

If not now, then when?

The Mother rises from the desk.

She sits on the sofa and holds the Son. His tawny hair smells like sweat. This is because, so often, he tucks it up against her breast. It feels comforting, to him and to her.

His sternum juts out. He is far too thin.

Still, he is happy. His voice is soft, like the distant chirping of crickets in the night.

5:15p.m.

An hour later, the Mother tells the Son that they need to go to the clinic.

He acquiesces.

The Mother is able to get the needle in with his doctor's coaching. He receives the fluids.

They return home.

He eats. The Mother is satisfied.

This treatment may be helpful.

8:32p.m.

The Son begins to vomit.

Frustration and anger arise in the Mother's mind. How relieved she had been after the doctor had reassured them. Now, the Son is getting sick all over the floorboards.

She finds her breath.

She holds his head tenderly, until he finishes.

She wipes the mess away with a sturdy paper towel and tosses it into the garbage bin beside the kitchen stove.

This garbage bin used to be a clothing hamper. It is plastic and brightly flowered. It is as cheerful in receiving the garbage, as it would be if a diamond were tossed into it.

When the Son is comfortably resting in bed, the Mother returns to the kitchen. She calms herself by cooking.

She steams blocks of tofu with garlic and ginger.

She wastes no time, energy, or ginger.

She sautés scallion, cabbage, and *shitake* mushroom, and then slices the tofu into thick, square strips. She heats pancakes. She spreads dollops of plum sauce.

The cooking is a meditation.

The lights are out early.

January 20, 2010

8:03a.m.

Today is a good day, because it is an off-day. This is not a treatment day.

The Son has stopped vomiting. He eats well.

The Mother squeezes fresh orange juice for him. She thinks of Tang and Sunny Delight.

She remembers her days at summer camp.

Sunburnt kids play Capture the Flag in an expansive field. Everyone is smiling.

Ceramic mermaids and tic-tac-toe boards are being painted in vibrant colors. Glitter glue abounds.

She is ready for a peaceful day.

Still, the Son seems tired. He wanders off to lie down by himself. He doesn't mind if the Mother sits with him, but he doesn't ask for her, either.

Perhaps this means that he is preparing to die, that he is surrendering.

The Mother is now convinced that this treatment is no good. The Son had been energetic until today.

His doctor has said that miracles can happen with this treatment. He could live for years.

In this moment, the Mother doesn't believe his doctor. A part of her thinks that the Son might live longer without the treatment.

Resentment arises.

His doctor has never been on these fluids. His doctor probably has no idea how they make him feel, why he vomits, why he is weakening.

The Mother wonders whether or not his doctor has ever seen anyone live for years with this treatment. Perhaps, that's just her line. Maybe, this is what she says to everyone, to get them to accept the treatment.

The rising resentment adds to her suffering over his condition.

She remembers talking with her student about the fourth step. Resentment may be the root of suffering, but what now is the cause of this resentment?

What is my weakness?

The Mother's weakness in this case is a feeling of helplessness.

She has held the Son since he was just weeks old. She cared for him, as he grew. Now, she can do nothing, as he grows sick and dies.

Must I sit back and watch him die?

With this question in mind, the Mother acknowledges that she is not a doctor. His doctor may know better than she what the Son's prognosis will be.

The Mother likes his doctor, even as she questions the effectiveness of the treatment. His doctor is intelligent and kind.

10:46a.m.

The Son considers the option to discontinue treatment.

He says that he doesn't want it.

The Mother respects his right to make this decision. Even so, she is concerned.

Is quitting treatment really in his best interest?

She, too, doubts the treatment, though she fears giving it up.

There is the risk that he may steadily decline as a result of discontinuing treatment. The Mother worries that he might suddenly get very sick. The possibilities of nausea, dehydration, and seizures loom.

If this illness gets out of control, how could they go back to his doctor and tell her, "We

29

didn't follow your treatment plan, but please can you help us now?"

Then again, if his doctor can't help now, how would she be able to help then?

The Son thinks that he will be alright without medical attention.

The Mother is not so sure. Even so, she realizes that the Son is frightened.

The situation seems hopeless, to both of them.

He is sure to die. The main questions now are when, and how. Would further treatment prolong a life of enjoyable quality or one of increased suffering?

Considering the options is exhausting.

The Mother prays for the Son to heal.

Today, there are no fluids to give.

3:30p.m.

The Mother has a meeting scheduled with a doctor at a nearby hospital.

She offers meditation workshops on the inpatient psychiatry ward there. The hospital is considering introducing the workshops to their outpatient program.

The Mother waits in a plain white conference room.

After a few minutes, the doctor appears. She wears a bright smile and a silk scarf tied around her hair.

They share mint tea in her office.

"You are a Sufi?" the Mother asks.

This doctor corrects her. "I am a student of Sufism." Then, she tells the Mother that she experiences a personal relationship with the Lord.

"You could share this with the patients," the Mother says.

"Oh no," this doctor says. "What would I tell them?"

"Just what you told me," the Mother says. "It's beautiful."

This doctor thinks that the patients would not respect her as a clinician if she talked about her relationship with the Lord.

The Mother wonders why. She agrees to lead the spirituality group, because she comes from "the outside," looks the part, and lives the life.

On the subway ride home, the Mother wonders what the Son's doctor might tell them about the treatment, if she were not concerned with being a clinician.

5:17p.m.

The Son meets the Mother at the front door with a grin. He does not let the Mother in on what is making him smile. He has found some kind of private joke with the universe, with his condition.

He is up and around again.

The side-effects of the treatment seem to have worn off.

January 21, 2010

3:35p.m.

No treatment.

No needles.

Just prayer, meditation, and quiet time together.

January 22, 2010

10:32a.m.

The Mother and the Son visit his doctor.

The Mother asks her, "Have you ever seen anyone live for years on this treatment?"

His doctor admits that the usual prognosis is six months.

"To a year," she adds quickly. "Six months to a year."

The Mother tells her how sick the fluids are making the Son.

His doctor suggests that he start taking a low dose of Xanax, so that he can tolerate the treatments.

He says, "No."

He does not want to live his last months, weeks, or days fogged over by tranquilizers.

His doctor says that there is nothing else that she knows to offer.

They receive his doctor's blessings to discontinue treatment.

10:45a.m.

The Son goes back to being his usual wildman self.

The Mother knows that he will die one day. Maybe soon. Maybe within two weeks without treatment, his doctor says.

But for now, they are happy.

7:49p.m.

Are we in denial?

January 23, 2010

2:00p.m.

The Mother meets a friend for tea. They go to a rustic French café where hot drinks are served in large, colorful bowls.

They discuss the Son's treatment.

They discuss "Don't Know."

This friend is a Zen meditation teacher.

"Every moment is fresh," she says. "There is no 'I.'"

They breathe together at the wooden table, amongst neighbors who are enjoying croissants and conversation.

"Just sit," this friend says. "Be in your body. Let the answer arise."

They can talk about anything, or they can sit together in silence. They are good friends.

People holding children's hands and shopping bags stroll past the picture window that opens out onto the street.

Life continues.

A sense of stillness arises.

4:49p.m.

The Mother returns home to find the Son lounging by an open window. He says that he is now ready to move forward with the treatment.

He has been considering the options, himself. He understands that the treatment may be helpful and reduce the suffering of his illness, even as the treatment may have side effects.

The Mother is relieved. This feels like the right decision. They will do what they can to extend his life, to keep him comfortable.

She calls his doctor and tells her that they are willing to try again.

January 24, 2010

3:25p.m.

A nurse comes over to help with the Son's treatment.

She is broad and sturdy, as if she had been raised on a farm. The Mother half-expects her to offer them bottles full of milk, still warm from the cow.

She doesn't. She is here to help with the needles.

The Son says he wants to follow through with this treatment, but when it comes down to it, he panics at the sight of the needle.

This time, the Mother is playing "the good guy." She is not the one piercing him with the needle. She is the one holding him and breathing with him.

She tells him that everything will be okay. The platitude is meaningless, yet these words are somehow comforting to both of them.

The Son wanders off to lie down after the treatment. The Mother sits with him. He doesn't vomit.

She steams rice and vegetables, and boils water for tea. He eats.

For now, he is here.

January 25, 2010

4:30p.m.

Today, the Mother is a half-hour late to the hospital where she teaches. She hopes that the occupational therapist will have gone home. Of course, he is the first person she sees when she arrives.

She had left a hurried phone message for him.

"Sorry. I'm running late. Something unavoidable came up."

The "something unavoidable" was that she'd slept until 3:30p.m. that afternoon. She is exhausted by worry over the Son's treatment, wiped out by the fear of losing him.

Her colleague is fine with the late arrival. He smiles, says it's great to see her, and gathers everyone for the meditation.

This is the detox ward.

The patients circle up in plastic chairs.

There is nothing to hide. All have hit rock bottom.

The group talks about how life is not "normal." Unexpected things happen.

Circumstances that may not be what we would choose arise unbidden.

Still, we can find structure and support through right action, through right intention.

Someone is dying. We feel helpless.

Still, we can ground ourselves through small acts of kindness. We remain competent.

There is no need for heroics.

We may not be able to save a slowly dwindling life.

We can, however, stay present with compassion and tenderness. So, we surrender to what we cannot control. In saying *yes* to dying, we are saying *yes* to life, as it appears in this moment.

We need not hold on tightly to what we love. In fact, we cannot.

When we let go, we find the space to breathe freely again. We find the space to be real, together.

January 26, 2010

8:49 p.m.

Emotional burnout.
Exhaustion.

January 28, 2010

3:49p.m.

The Mother sits through several hours of meetings at the United Nations. The conference room overlooks a courtyard with flags that hail from countries around the world. The view is beautiful.

She pretends to be alright.

Am I not really alright?

Nothing needs to be said. The Mother sits at the long, rectangular table. She listens, and she smiles. It's enough.

After the meeting wraps up, the representatives of various international charities shake hands and wish each other, "Happy New Year."

Will anyone else be going home to a dying son?

January 29, 2010

3:45p.m.

Today is pleasantly uneventful.

The Son likes to sit in a bamboo chair at the small writing table in front of a window. The window faces south.

He gazes down into the courtyard of a wine shop, and out over the grace of bare tree branches reaching into sky.

In the late afternoons, he watches the sun set.

His needs are simple. He is contented with empty hands.

In his presence, the Mother feels complete.

7:59p.m.

Early in the evening, the Mother stops by a neighboring church to drop off some paperwork.

She edits a literary magazine. The magazine's copy editor teaches English to Hispanic women at this church.

The Mother leaves the upcoming issue of the magazine for the copy editor in the minster's box.

Industrious, the copy editor will mark up the manuscript with her red pencil, reminding the Mother of the finer grammatical points not taught in college composition classes.

The Mother feels lucky to work with her.

In the chapel down the hall, a small group is rehearsing chamber music.

The music calls to her.

The Mother lies down on the worn red carpet in the wood-paneled room next door. Light shines in from the hallway.

She listens to the song of the string quartet.

Nobody knows that she is here.

In this moment, there are no responsibilities. She listens to the music, without needing to do anything. She feels relief.

January 30, 2010

1:49p.m.

The Son's nurse arrives to help with his treatment. She is punctual, the kind of person who can be counted on to show up when she says she will.

She is less matter-of-fact than stolidly caring.

She is not squeamish about needles. She pushes the needle through the Son's translucent skin without a second thought. She starts the fluids running from a turgid bag that the Mother has hung from the solid edge of a large, gilt picture frame.

The Mother holds the Son in her arms.

He begins to tremble. She rocks him gently.

This may be how he dies one day. In my arms.

Tears come.

Tears come, because they purify the heart.

January 31, 2010

8:16p.m.

The Mother walks softly from her office into the temple. The altar is lit with tiny candles. They flicker in frosted glass cups.

Quietly, she begins to dance.

She stretches out with grace. She bends over her long, straight legs.

Now, she is looking at the room upside down. This is an unusual view.

The Mother contemplates the day.

This afternoon, a friend called. She asked how the Mother was doing, how the Son was doing.

The Mother told her friend on the telephone this afternoon that everything was fine.

Why did I say this afternoon that everything was fine?

The Mother decides to somersault. It will be fun, she thinks.

She squats down on the floor. Her long hair flows like a river around her shoulders.

She discovers that she is afraid. She can't let go to go over.

Why could I not open up to somebody who cares?

Perhaps, there had been no time to express the feelings, so like quicksand or mercury, the subtleties that elude words because we do not fully understand them ourselves, though they are of our own mind, of our own heart, of our own salt tears.

So often, a question is asked because it should be asked, asked in a breezy manner, asked without anyone's really wanting the answer, asked without the generous gift of time and space for a searching response, one that wanders and explores and eventually discovers and is able to express a deeper truth.

How am I doing?

Even the best of friends may shy away from discussing what we cannot control but what we know must in the end be each of our fates—this mysterious death, this unknowable transformation.

The Mother tries to somersault again and again, and she can't. She remembers being fearless in a kindergarten gymnastics class.

What will I hold onto?

Finally, she somersaults.

She is a child, again.

Her grandfather has died on Thanksgiving Day. The holiday party at her home in Los Angeles is cancelled, so that this white haired man whom she adored can be burned to ash in Miami.

She will fly across the country on a plane with her mother, whose father this was.

She will ride for the first time in a limousine, on the way to the funeral home. In this long and exaggerated car, she will plan his eulogy, for she will speak at the podium of what a wonderful grandfather he was. She will not break down in public. She is composed, as she ever is, and she is wearing party shoes.

Years later, at her great-aunt's funeral, she will indeed break down in public, for her almighty mother figure is being taken from her in a draped but strangely shiny box.

She will be wearing the dress her great-aunt loved, a stunningly simple black crepe number, and again she will be wearing party shoes.

Her great-aunt would undoubtedly have said, as she did so often, "Darling, keep looking like that."

People she barely knows will smile kindly at her. There will be cameras everywhere, from which she will duck and turn, and her family will ask her please, to stop crying, or at least to leave the room, for no one else at this elegant funeral is crying.

Later, they will console her kindly, with hot chocolate in the hotel dining room. They adore her, though no one understands why she is so emotional.

Now, she dances in her temple. In an adjoining room, the Son is dying. She cannot save him.

The situation feels absurd. There might as well be an orangutan swinging from the ceiling beams, chattering and scratching at his fleas, in the midst of this all. How incongruous it is to love someone such that you would do anything for him, and yet to be able to do nothing in the midst of his suffering, to sit by as he slowly and surely dies.

What is there to do in the absurdity of this situation but roll around on the floor?

She rolls forwards and backwards a few times, somersaulting like the child she was in her kindergarten gymnastics class.

Then, she lies down on her back.

She is aware that the Son is dying.

Her emotions feel like more than she can handle. She cannot name them, but she can feel them.

Help me.

She cries. It's a release. To cry allows her to continue.

She begins again to dance.

She stands and moves, contracting and expanding, reaching into infinity with grace.

The breath is free.

The mind is relaxed.

In an adjoining room, the Son sleeps peacefully.

February 1, 2010

12:53a.m.

The Mother awakens in the middle of the night.

She is startled by anxiety.

Why are his illness and treatment so upsetting?

In understanding what gives our emotions their power, we find relief.

When the Mother was a child, she dreamt that her teddy bear was lost. She couldn't find him anywhere. Then, she wandered into the forest.

There, she came upon the bear, wrapped in a cocoon that hung like a hammock between two aged trees.

The bear was dead. He had wandered off by himself, because he knew that he was going to die, and he had died.

Upon waking, the Mother told her father about the dream.

He said, "The teddy bear is a part of you. The dream means that a part of you is dying, the part of you that needs a teddy bear. Maybe the dream means that you're growing up."

Her father had brought this teddy bear back with from London, where he had attended his own father's funeral.

The Mother felt the loss of this gruff grandfather's death, even with the bear in her arms.

Now, she rises from a corner of the floor, where the moon casts gentle shadows. She enters an adjoining room to watch the Son as he sleeps.

He is small and innocent.

She holds him in her gaze. This time together is precious.

The Son awakens suddenly. His eyes are wide.

When something's important, he says so.

When he found out he was dying, he said, "I don't want to see anybody else. I only want to spend time with you."

So, the Mother asks him now about this treatment.

He groans and turns away. He doesn't want to talk about medical procedures. It is the middle of the night.

The Mother gazes up at the bright moon.

When he is really dying, there will be nothing I can do. This child trusts me to care for him now, but at the moment of death, I will not be able to save him.

The Mother feels helpless.

This struggle for control is meaningless in the vast cycle of birth and death, she thinks, for what is born must die.

She remembers a man she once saw standing on a beach. In the distance, he was no more than a tiny figure against a vast and darkening sky.

Perhaps there is a beauty to man's insignificance in the face of nature. How blessed we are to be even a small part of it all, this glorious creation.

The moon shines, unfazed.

Death is a natural part of the life cycle. If we lived in the forest or even on a farm, we would have learned this as children. Instead, we grow up sheltered, such that nature's ways are shocking.

The moon is steadily luminescent, reflecting light in the darkness.

3:55p.m.

The Mother arrives on the detox ward.

The first patient she encounters smiles and says, "Who are you supposed to be?"

"I don't know," she says.

It's a good question. Who are any of us supposed to be?

A man with long black hair notices that the Mother wears motorcycle boots under the robes.

He says, "I didn't know those boots were back in style."

The patients make her laugh.

They are off to a good start.

7:32p.m.

The Mother leaves her slushy boots at the door.

Inside, the rooms are warm and the lamps are lit. The Son is up and about. He is in good spirits.

She tells the Son that he's her baby.

He pretends to be an infant.

He mimics a child's cry, opening his mouth wide and waving his fists.

Waaa.Waaa.

They both laugh.

Then, he's off to putter about. He tends to the abandoned cats that they shelter, patting and crooning to them. One has been rescued from a church basement. Others were cared for by people who became ill or homeless. Now, they curl up in baskets, leap up onto windowsills, and sleep at the foot of the Son's bed.

He straightens his bedding, before lying down to rest.

The Mother sits at the window, and prays.

8:45p.m.

About Lazarus—

When the Mother's grandfather died, she prayed that he be raised again.

Clearly, to raise someone from the dead is possible. Christ raised Lazarus with a few words, calling him to come out of the tomb, after he had been dead for days.

And so, Lazarus did come out, to the joy of his two sisters.

The Mother had believed that her grandfather could be raised from the dead.

The living Christ is more present now than he has ever been.Why then do people die, today?

Her grandfather did not rise from the dead. Instead, he was burnt to ash.

At this point, the Mother began to lose faith in the Church.

Why should God want us to suffer, when Christ could reach down his heavenly hand to grant our loved ones life again?

Sitting before the window, she contemplates the way our loved ones are raised.

Through the sacrifice on the Cross, we are forgiven, such that the Spirit overcomes the body's frailties, and even death. In dying on our Cross, the soul is perfected, such that we can keep company with the saints and angels, with the ascended Lord himself, with the infinite glory that is the truth of being.

For the way that I turned away from the Church after my grandfather's death, I am truly sorry.

She realizes now that she did not appreciate the blessings in her life during those early naive years. She considers how she suffered for this lack of faith.

She is thankful to be able to pray and to feel the presence of the Lord, again.

She once asked a priest why, if Christ could raise the dead, he only did this for a few people, why this doesn't happen today.

The priest said that the miracle wasn't the point. Christ performed miracles to get our attention, to show us that the power of the Father was within him, so that we would listen to his teachings. His teachings are what is important. They us how to live our lives.

Another priest explained things further. He said that we don't know why people die. Death is a mystery, like so many things that happen during life. It is important to give thanks for the abundant blessings that we do receive. We will be given more than we could ever imagine in the life to come, when there will be no sickness, aging, or death.

Christ gives us the strength to continue through our present challenges. "Our faith is tested daily, though only to make us stronger," said the priest.

Here at the window, the Mother gives thanks for the blessing of the Son in her life. She will try to love others, just as she loves him.

Note: Consider this. If everyone's dead loved ones were raised, the earth would be incredibly overpopulated.

February 2, 2010

7:15p.m.

The Mother struggles with more work than she can handle. Really, her struggle is resistance of the mind.

She walks from the desk, through the office door, down a small hallway, and into the temple.

She begins to dance, again. The movements are long, slow, and peaceful.

She offers her dance to the awakening of all beings.

7:46p.m.

Can we make an offering of anything we do?
Consider ordinary action.
Flip a switch. The room lights up.
Offer it. May all beings be liberated.
Enjoy a piece of cake after dinner. There's little virtue in that. Cake is not nutritious. Still, it tastes good. Offer that enjoyment to all beings. Let it be a rare treat.

When we do something imperfectly, when we try and then we fail, we can offer that effort.

What if we do something that we regret?

We make a mistake. We realize that we have made a mistake. We are sorry.

We make an offering of making that mistake, of realizing that mistake and of trying to resolve it.

In this way, perhaps we never do anything indelibly wrong. We learn from our mistakes and offer our attempts at reparation to the awakening of all beings.

We can be forgiven.

8:43p.m.

The Son's nurse arrives for his treatment.

He says outright that he doesn't want to do this, today.

He doesn't like this nurse. He says so in front of her.

His nurse handles the rejection well. She tries to smile at him.

The Mother listens to his complaints.

She explains that this nurse is doing them a favor by making home visits, that she charges only what they can afford.

His eyes well up with tears, and he retreats to another room.

The Mother is ready to call it quits with this treatment. They will just enjoy the time together.

His nurse tells the Mother that sometimes, there are treatments that people need. They don't like them, but they receive them anyway.

She is firm.

She finds the Son huddled in bed and asks him to try one more time.

He is pleased by her efforts to talk with him.

The treatment is not so bad. It takes only a few minutes out of the day.

He feels better immediately afterwards.

February 3, 2010

6:07p.m.

Today is a day of back-to-back meetings. There is no time to type notes between conferences.

In addition to every other duty, the Mother now needs to write a paper. The paper will reflect what the working group she chairs plans to do this year at the United Nations.

9:28p.m.

Dinner is paper-wrapped burritos from a neighborhood *taqueria*. The Mother is tired. Even so, she and the Son talk about his nurse.

The Son says that he is intimidated by her. She pushes the needles too hard.

The Mother understands that the treatment may be uncomfortable and frightening. It must seem that his nurse is up to no good. Anyone in his small, fleecy slippers might assume the same thing.

The purpose of this treatment, however, is to keep him comfortable. This is why his nurse visits, to help with the treatment and to keep him comfortable. Perhaps they can ask her to be more gentle with the needles.

The Son wants to continue his treatment. He feels better and enjoys his simple life. He would, however, like a different nurse. He prefers the nurse who wears wacky green glasses and calls him "little guy." She visits once in a while when his regular nurse cannot.

The Mother likes this wacky nurse, too. She wishes that they could hire her. This nurse, however, is less reliable. She is often late or needs to reschedule the visit. She once spoke about having stopped for lunch to meet friends at a bar.

The Son insists that he likes her better. Perhaps, he would like to go to the bar with her.

The Mother sits quietly, gazing into his clear green eyes, so like sea glass.

Finally, the Son agrees.

Wondering if, when, or how his nurse might show up is stressful. He, too, wants to be sure that he will receive treatment on schedule, as planned.

He is willing to continue with the sturdy and reliable nurse.

He straightens his striped blanket. He cracks a smile and acknowledges that she tries to be friendly.

She will be back, tomorrow.

February 4, 2010

7:42p.m.

The Mother studies the *37 Practices of the Bodhisattva*, by Ngulchu Thogme Zangpo.

Even if someone for whom one has cared
as tenderly as one's own child
considers one to be a enemy,
to cherish that being, as a mother
does a very sick child
is the bodhisattva's practice. 16

Consider how different life would be were we to care for all beings as we care for a beloved child who is dying. Perhaps, we can appreciate in good health that this time together is a precious gift.

8:06p.m.

The Son's nurse arrives to help with his treatment.

She and the Mother try to make the Son comfortable on the couch, with pillows of every shape and color. He rests his head on a cushion that has been embroidered with a giant sunflower.

He doesn't like the treatment. He says so boldly.

His nurse agrees with him. The treatment is uncomfortable.

Next week, they will redo his bloodwork to find out whether or not it is helping.

February 5, 2010

10:32a.m.

The Mother receives an e-mail about a woman who is passing. She is a sundancer, one who sacrifices in the yearly Native American ceremony for the good of generations yet to come. Prayers are requested for her, as she prepares to journey into Spirit.

This is a beautiful way to think about death—as a transition from the body into a state of complete and formless absorption, as transformation into that for which there are no words or concepts.

Death is indeed a journey into Spirit.

12:06p.m.

The Mother steps into the elevator. A neighbor greets her.

He carries his dachshund, whom he is taking for a walk, in the crook of his arm.

He is an actor. His white hair sweeps dramatically back from his face. He speaks with concentration and resonance.

He says, "You look lovely. You give me strength."

Then, he asks if the Mother will say prayers for someone who is dying.

"Yes," she says. "Of course I will."

If only you knew how much I am struggling, how much I too need prayers for someone who is dying.

Another neighbor rushes into the elevator. She realizes that she has forgotten to remove her bike helmet.

She looks at the Mother and says, "Thank the Lord that somebody's on the ball."

Yes, I am on the ball. I am ever balancing, practicing equanimity in a world of change, as are we all.

The Mother is in a quiet mood, today.

Maybe encouraging the Son to continue treatment is wrong. After all, he is terminally ill.

On the other hand, the treatment now seems to be helping.

She has no answers. She does not feel like a teacher, today.

Still, she is on her way to offer meditation workshops on two psychiatry wards.

Perhaps she is going onto the wards more as a visiting friend than anything else.

She plans to read from the *Katha Upanishad*. In this scripture, Death is a teacher—Death with his face of light and dark cloak, Death who enlightens a young boy, Nachiketa, sent too soon to die. Death then returns him to the world of the living.

> *Two sip at the waters of truth.*
> *One craves the result of worldly deed,*
> *tasting both the bitter and the sweet.*
> *The other has entered the sacred*
> *cave of the heart, the Lord's abode.*
> *They are as shadow and light—*
> *the worldly one parched with insatiable desire,*
> *the merged soul immersed in truth.*   I.3.i

How is it that we awaken from the duality of sweet and bitter, of likes and dislikes, of life and death? Such experience is relevant to what any of us may live through.

Depression or anxiety arise from the mind-set of duality, from grasping at pleasure and rejecting pain, from the insistence that things in our lives need to be one way and not another.

When we are able to taste of the sweet and the bitter in this world with equanimity, the mind stabilizes.

Truly, we need taste neither. Identified with the Lord, the soul looks on, needing nothing from this world, and lives in freedom.

The patients are like empty cups. They are able to receive what is offered to them.

They do not purport to know anything. So, they are open to new ideas. This is why they have powerful experiences with the poetry and with the meditation. Sitting with them is joyful.

1:15p.m.

On the television in the day room, a murder mystery is blaring. The Mother receives the patients' permission to turn the movie off.

The walls of the day room are papered with colorful drawings.

A young girl points to one of them. "That's mine," she says, proudly. "It's a symbol of who I am."

The girl explains that she still feels innocent, even with all that she has put herself and her loved ones through. She is hopeful for renewal.

She and the Mother pray, together.

Meanwhile, the rest of the patients circle up for the workshop.

A bipolar man who has just been fired from his job joins the group. He has lost his job, because he has trouble managing his coworkers. He is manic and talkative. He discusses relationship in terms of laying tile. This is what's needed, today:

Clear the ground of debris. Put the same kind of glue onto both the floor and the tile. It must be just right—not too dry and not too fresh—the same on both sides. Then, when they are put together, the bond is such that they will never come apart.

His insights are useful to everyone. Each one struggles with maintaining relationship, with rebuilding trust.

The Mother does not read from the *Katha Upanishad*. The group does not discuss the teachings of Death. They explore awakening in a different context. They talk about the foundation of relationship and bonding. This is what's needed, today.

February 6, 2010

11:07a.m.

Today is peaceful.

The Mother listens to the hush of cars passing in the street, to a lone bird chirping, to the breath.

She could recite prayers, but it would disturb the stillness.

The Son seems to feel at peace, in a way that he hasn't before. She can't say what or why, but something has shifted. He has accepted his situation.

6:30p.m.

The Mother attends a teaching on *sunyata*, emptiness.

She sits with a friend, a Buddhist nun who lives in a small community, upstate.

The two are like mirror images. This friend is bold. She brings the Mother out of her shell of insecurities. In turn, the Mother listens and understands when this friend has been hurt.

They bow, take refuge, and chant the *Heart Sutra*.

The *geshe* begins to speak.

Subject emptiness.

The mind changes in its perceptions. Our ideas about a person or circumstance may not be consistent over time.

Object emptiness.

A person or circumstance will be experienced differently by different people. The object is not solid. It is not all one way or another.

We can think of this worldly impermanence as the potential for change.

When subject and object come together, we cannot say that a situation is good, bad, or anything at all. We open beyond our immediate personal reaction to take in the full experience.

The mind is empty of judgement. Awareness is expansive and free.

The teaching is what is needed.

Afterwards, the Mother kneels before the *geshe* and supplicates his opinion on medical treatment. She asks whether it right or wrong to encourage someone to continue with treatment, if he does not want to continue. She has faith in this teacher, in his true wisdom and great compassion.

The *geshe* encourages her to look at the long term result, rather than the short term result. If the treatment is helping, then the long term result is that the Son's life will be extended. Perhaps this benefit outweighs any brief discomfort that he feels.

He is a kind teacher. He listens carefully. He answers every question.

8:37p.m.

The telephone rings.

Minutes later, there is a knock at the door. The Son's nurse arrives.

His treatment takes place in complete silence.

He doesn't mind it this time. He is happy.

February 7, 2010

10:32a.m.

The Mother and the Son watch a movie about the life of an Indian saint who spent much of his life in silence.

The Mother feels close to this silent saint.

With spiritual masters, it makes no difference whether a teacher is in the body or not. The masters remain ever-present. Their presence may become even stronger, when it is no longer limited by form.

This silent saint is one of her greatest inspirations. When he was a young boy, his father died. The family was separated, and he went to live with an uncle.

Sometime later, he was gripped by the fear of his own death. This shock drove him inward. He began to explore within himself what might remain after his was carried to the burning grounds. He realized himself as the immortal Spirit.

Soon after, he gave up his schooling and became a *sadhu*. He descended to meditate in a temple basement.

There he became fully absorbed in the bliss of silence.

In time, devotees began to visit this awakened youth.

His silently radiant presence transformed many.

The Mother and the Son sit silently together and watch the film.

11:52p.m.

The sun shines through the window, warming the room. Light falls across the papers piled upon the desk.

How best do we balance our time between stillness and service?

Several copies of the *Bhagavad Gita* are stacked up on the desk. Some of the volumes are slim and elegant. Others are thick with commentary, with pages that smell of newsprint.

Although the teachings are thousands of years old, they remain as current as the daily news, for they are universal.

In this scripture, the Lord reveals the secrets of action and inaction.

One who sees inaction in action
and action in inaction
is wise among seekers.   4.18

Inaction in action. The mind may be still, even as the body moves. We surrender personal desire to become an instrument of divine grace. We offer the fruit of the action. We are one with the moment, with the action, with the Lord. Such is inaction in action.

Meanwhile, for one who sits still but meditates with a wandering mind, there is action in inaction. When neglecting or avoiding duty, there is action in inaction.

Still, with right intention, there may be service in contemplative stillness. We pray for others. We share vibration through meditation. We shirk no duty but allow doing to fall away, as do the petals of a blossom when the fruit is ripe.

In service, the quality of mind matters more than the external appearance of action or inaction.

2:17p.m.

Consider inaction in action. We might also describe this as stillness in action. It is an inner stillness, or a stillness of mind. Perhaps this is the emptiness of mind. So, we find great compassion in action. We become selfless in action.

The Mother remembers the conversation with the contractor on the psychiatry ward, about the tile and the floor.

The ground is cleared of debris. Object emptiness.

The tile too must have a clear surface. Subject emptiness.

Debris is thought-elaboration. Thought-elaboration exists only in the mind.

When the debris is cleared, the mind relaxes into silence.

Maybe there is no glue. Maybe there is more of a magnetic bond than a clinging desire that brings us into union with truth.

The tile becomes one with the clear ground.

The individual becomes one with the universal.

One is inseparable from the one. One has always been the one. There has never been another.

Such is stillness in stillness.

The mind is quiet.

The desk is still stacked with work, but there is no feeling of being busy.

The Son sits in prayer.

Both the Son and the Mother are at peace.

February 8, 2010

10:35a.m.

Things go back to "normal," today.
The mind is quiet. The heart is contented.

1:30p.m.

A friend from the United Nations visits to give the Son an acupressure treatment. She is a healer.

She shows up eager and smiling.

It doesn't matter whether someone is "dying" or not. We don't know what may happen. We offer everything possible for healing.

There is, of course, a difference between cure and healing.

Cure is a remedy for the physical illness. It may come through medicine, mechanism, or surgery, as well as faith. Cure alleviates or eliminates disease symptoms.

Healing is spiritual. Healing is being able to understand and accept what is happening with the illness. So, we adapt to this new way of living.

Healing is about discovering renewed connection with ourselves, with others, and with the transcendent. Perhaps we find healing in connecting to nature or the arts, as well. Healing is a deepening of awareness, an awakening to this blessed present moment.

The Son sits, quiet and solemn, awaiting this new holistic treatment.

The Mother's friend lays her hands on him. Her fingertips move intuitively. Soon, she feels an energy blockage. This is where the illness is. She works for nearly an hour, but she is unable to clear the energy.

Disappointment arises. The Mother and the Son believe in miracles. They had hoped for a cure. Still, they are glad to have invited this healer into their lives.

Now, they receive her invitation to accept what they cannot change. All three sit back and join hands. Healing may mean that we accept dying as a natural part of life of the life cycle.

When someone is dying, we can reflect with our loved one on the roles that we have played throughout this life, together—at work and in relationship, in offering small acts of kindness to each other.

What, now, is the role of dying?

It is possible to be emotionally mature at this stage of the game. We can still smile, even as we may shed tears. There is a dignity to dying.

We may ask ourselves what the dying one's legacy will be. We reflect upon how this being has grown through a lifetime and brought transformation to the community.

What is the impact of the Son's life?

We consider our beliefs about the soul's destination after it departs from the body.

We appreciate how precious our time together is.

We give thanks for this shared experience.

5:45p.m.

The Mother returns home directly after the meditation workshop at the hospital. She returns early to spend time with the Son, rather than attending this evening's Buddhist Council meeting.

She could bring him with her to the meeting, but he prefers to relax. The Son draws the Mother into his stillness. They find healing, together. This time is precious.

February 9, 2010

11:07 a.m.

The day's schedule is clear. There is nowhere to be but here, at home, together.

The morning seems busy, anyway. This is because the mind is busy. The Mother is working hard to distract herself from the Son's illness.

She is disappointed that the energy blockage could not be cleared.

The Son, too, is quiet.

They consider his impending departure. Neither of them wants to be separated.

They breathe.

They listen.

They sit quietly together.

They let go of the idea that he is dying.

They appreciate that he is living, here.

They give thanks that he is living, now.

The Mother and the Son enjoy sitting across from each other at the desk, without the shadow of impending loss. They are simply present together, in this moment.

She lays her hand on his.

The rest of the day is peaceful and productive.

Life feels right.

February 10, 2010

5:26 p.m.

A snowstorm hits and lasts all day.

This snowstorm is nothing compared to the snowstorms the Mother experienced when she attended college up in Ithaca, New York. The waterfalls there would freeze in mid-air, as they poured from the rocky gorges.

This snowstorm is nothing compared to the blizzard the Mother experienced when she first moved to New York City, when schools and offices were closed for days, when snow piled six feet high on either side of the streets, when her college roommate stayed over at her apartment because she could not get home after work, when they painted their nails metallic blue.

Even so, everything in the city shuts down, today. Schools are cancelled. Businesses close early.

The Mother sends an e-mail querying about the status of this evening's meditation workshop.

Yes, the hospital suggests that she stay home.

The Mother lights the lamps.

The Son decides to make popcorn.

The Mother steams milk for hot chocolate.

There are no expectations on this sudden holiday.

February 13, 2010

8:16 p.m.

The Mother and a friend are joking around online. They send a barrage of e-mails back and forth. They might as well be on the telephone, but they are not.

The telephone rings.

"Hellooo," the Mother says. She is in a silly mood.

The woman on the other end tells the Mother that she may be dying. She has just had emergency surgery. She is looking for someone to visit her, to discuss spiritual teachings.

The Mother remembers joking around in India at the *ashram* juice bar, and her teacher's words. "Get serious. Get to work."

The woman on the telephone is a Buddhist. The Mother explains that she studied in a Hindu *ashram*.

The woman says that she would like the Mother to visit. She lives in Brooklyn.

They plan to meet later in the week. The woman sounds relieved and happy.

February 16, 2010

10:42a.m.

The Mother's uncle calls.

His son, her cousin, has just been discharged from drug rehab.

He isn't back at college. He was found trying to cut his wrists in the shower.

He is being transferred to a psychiatric hospital.

3:17p.m.

The Mother arrives on time for the meditation workshop on the detox ward. She enjoys the patients' company. She feels blessed to be working with them. She hopes to offer them a useful teaching.

Today, there is a boy in the group who says that he isn't able to meditate. He has attended one meditation workshop elsewhere, and meditation isn't possible for him.

True to his word, he gets up in the middle of the sitting to walk out the door.

The Mother stops him. She spot-checks his mind.

He is upset over someone who has just died. He doesn't know how to handle the feelings.

The Mother hugs this boy. Hugging seems the most effective thing to do in the moment, with the two of them standing in the doorway of a room where ten other patients and an occupational therapist are meditating in silence.

She embraces him out of compassion, as one loving human being to another.

Affection seems to help. Touch expresses caring that is beyond words.

He calms down. "What should I do, now?" he asks.

"What do you want to do?" the Mother says.

"You tell me," he says.

"Have a seat," she says.

The boy does, and meditates for the rest of the hour.

February 17, 2010

10:47a.m.

The Mother reads from the *Bhagavad Gita*. Months have passed since she has looked into the first chapter, the chapter on the disciple's confusion in the midst of the battlefield. The warrior prince is mired in doubt. Should he fight his teachers, friends, and family over land that is rightfully his father's, or should he retreat? What is the truly virtuous way to behave?

The Lord, his charioteer, explains that we cannot shirk our duty.

> *On who rejoices in the soul*
> *is satisfied in the soul. For him*
> *there is nothing to be done.*
> *In this world, there is nothing*
> *for him to gain or lose,*
> *and no one to impress.*
> *Like this wise one, do your duty*
> *without seeking result,*
> *for so doing you shall awaken.*   *3.17-19*

Life is not about choosing between battle or retreat. Life is about doing our best with what is in front of us.

This will be different for each of us—what we are here to do, our unique and necessary purpose. The path to truth varies according to our natural tendencies.

Our purpose here is not only to work but also to enjoy—to appreciate the beauty of creation, to participate fully with it.

Ultimately, we are each born to seek liberation.

Life guides us. Certain doors close and new ones open. We have only to accept the invitation.

Can we trust and relax? Can we say yes to a change in circumstance? Can we surrender to a loved one's dying?

3:30p.m.

Today is the day for the Son's blood test. The Mother bundles him up for the walk to his doctor's office, just a few blocks away.

They walk together, even though it is cold outside. Their footsteps crunch in the snow.

They both look away when his doctor brings out the needle.

For a moment, the Mother glances over at the tube that is slowly filling. The Son's blood is very red. It is the color of pomegranate or ruby, or fine red wine.

The Son begins to cry.

His doctor remains calm. She has straight blond hair and wears a starched white coat. She takes care of both the Son and the Mother.

As soon as they leave his doctor's office, the Son forgets about the blood test.

They reach home and hang their coats. The Mother's is saffron and hooded. The Son's is royal blue. Both coats drip with melting snowflakes.

The Mother shuts the closet door.

The Son's doctor will call with the test results, tomorrow.

He is smiling as he sits down in his favorite bamboo chair, by the window. He shifts to get comfortable. The straw seat creaks gently.

5:16p.m.

The Buddhist woman recovering from surgery, whom the Mother is supposed to visit, has left a voice-mail message.

Her doctor does not want anyone coming into her home, for fear of infection. She would like to reschedule their meeting.

The Mother looks forward to speaking with her, again.

The Son's blood test has been forgotten.

He expresses concern for this woman and encourages the Mother to call her.

February 18, 2010

5:07 p.m.

The Mother speaks with the Buddhist woman for nearly an hour by telephone. They share a good, solid talk.

This woman acknowledges that her doctor and family didn't feel comfortable with her having a stranger over to the house.

She and the Mother laugh about this. They don't feel like strangers to each other. They plan to speak again next week.

February 19, 2010

8:53p.m.

The Mother telephones her cousin.

He asks in a flat tone how she is doing.

He tells her with even less affect that he is fine.

Then, he hands the receiver over to his father, her uncle.

The Mother considers what to do next. Her cousin is completely shut down. She asks her uncle to put him back on the telephone.

This time, they talk about what's really going on—living in a fog, thinking that things will never get better, counting on friends who reject you, being questioned by uncaring counselors.

These are the trials that we go through to become superheroes, the Mother tells her cousin.

Her cousin agrees. He brightens.

They will speak again, tomorrow.

February 20, 2010

9:07p.m.

Today has been busy.

The Mother attends a morning meeting to formalize the meditation program at one hospital.

In the afternoon, she offers two workshops at another hospital.

When she returns home, she and her cousin speak again.

She cries when tonight's conversation ends.

The tears feel like a relief or release. She is sorry for what this cousin is going through. She is glad to have been able to connect with him.

She thinks of her teacher in India. For as long as people suffer, we must do whatever we can in service to their awakening.

When we realize our particular calling in service, this is our *svadharma*. We realize our life purpose in the heart.

February 26, 2010

10:39 a.m.

The Mother sleeps with her head on a book. Her teacher once said that if we do this, we will realize the wisdom in the scripture, and the source of that wisdom.

She sleeps with her head on the *Bhagavad Gita*. On the cover is a picture of the Lord, radiant against a splendid red background.

This morning she wakes up with her left ear suction-cupped to his feet.

I take refuge in the feet of the Lord.

In the *Bhagavad Gita*, the Lord teaches us how to awaken.

Rest your mind on me alone.
So will you live in me forever.　　　*12.8*

Devotion to the Lord purifies the mind. It is a bridge into silence.

February 27, 2010

5:25p.m.

The Mother speaks again with the Buddhist woman in Brooklyn. She is recovering well from the emergency surgery. She is out of imminent danger.

She is meditating regularly.

February 28, 2010

7:19 p.m.

The Mother lies on the floor all day and watches the light change. This is beauty.

February 29, 2010

12:49 p.m.

The Mother is waiting for the elevator in a local *ashram* bookstore. On the wall by the elevator door hang painted pictures of the awakened ones.

The Medicine Buddha is blue.

He is deep blue, beautiful blue, resonant blue.

Blue is the color of rain clouds.

Today, the Mother is here to teach on breaking the bounds of expectation.

In preparing for the workshop, the Son's dying has become the primary example.

She sits with a group of students in a room that is painted eggshell blue. There is the simultaneously sense of beauty and of fragility.

The shell that protects the developing bird must be broken for the little one to step out, to breathe, and to fly.

Death may be something like this.

The soul breaks through the bounds of form such that it can be free to expand into the infinite.

GRIEF

The death of a loved one is something that we will each live through. Caring for someone who is dying brings us to a place where we let go of expectation. So, we let go of doing. We surrender to the process. We surrender to the Lord.

This being has not died
like this,
before, and I
have never
witnessed his death,
before.
We gaze with infant eyes——
open,
curious.
We don't know
what's going to happen.
Whatever happens is just happening.

He is dying,
and we are liberated
from trying to change his dying,
because we cannot. We are liberated
from doing anything at all.

In becoming powerless,
we are liberated.
We hold the moment's
simple beauty, together.
Freedom and suffering are simultaneous.
So, there is no lasting truth to suffering.

I hold him.
I listen to him.
I love him,
as I never have before.

This moment is precious.

This is how we can live—
live fully,
live with bare awareness,
live open and engaged.

What's right
in front of you?
You've never seen this before.
You've never tasted, smelled, or heard
exactly like this,
before.

GRIEF

You've never felt this, before.
You have never
come into relationship
with the world,
quite like this.
And, it will never happen again.
Not quite like this.
Live like this.
Be no one and be one.

4:56p.m.

Gate Gate Paragate Parasamgate Bodhi Svaha

Beyond,
Beyond.
We'll go beyond.
We'll go together.
Beyond the beyond.
We offer mind
into the sunrise
of awakening.

March 15, 2010

11:07a.m.

The Mother wonders whether she may be having a panic attack. She's not sure what a panic attack is, but this feeling is strange.

The Son's impending death is today's reality. She doesn't want to lose him.

Her forehead is squinched up with worry. She can't catch her breath. She feels anxious.

He just can't die. I won't be able to handle it.

She remembers feeling this way after her great-aunt died.

Her great-aunt died suddenly.

She fell and hit her head after lunch. The next day, her life was finished. Unplugged.

A card the Mother had written to her lay ready to be mailed on the writing desk, when the news came that her great-aunt was dead.

Suddenly, the Mother was alone in the world.

Who will take care of me, now?

Such was the thought that arose in the mind when her great-aunt was carried away, on the shoulders of six pall bearers, after a grand funeral.

Always, it had been her great-aunt who bailed the Mother out, when she was sick, broke, or jobless.

"Tell me what kind of a job you want, and I'll help you get one," her great-aunt said, one winter when the Mother was in a slump.

"But I don't know what I'm meant to do with my life," said the Mother.

"Take a week. Think it over. Call and let me know," was the reply.

It was her great-aunt with whom the Mother spent holidays, feasting in hotel ballrooms and sharing song during intimate family gatherings.

"I want to give you your heart's desire," her great-aunt had once said, the week before Christmas.

The Mother can't remember how long the panic attacks lasted after her great-aunt died, but only that they began happening in public at her funeral.

And now the Son is dying.

How do these deaths compare? The great-aunt was like a mother to her. The Son is like the Mother's own child. Still, the feeling of loss is the same.

4:56p.m.

The Son eats, but he is losing weight. His silly striped pajamas hang loose on his frame.

Fear rises in the Mother's mind.

What will his test results show? I can't handle it if he's really going to die , now.

The Mother has lost almost as much weight as the Son.

She tries to take care of herself, but she isn't hungry and hasn't been exercising.

Instead of letting the stress go, she seems to have abandoned any stabilizing routine.

Because the Son is dying, there is the temptation to spend every waking minute at his bedside. The Mother does not know how long he will be with her. Every moment is precious.

Innate wisdom says that, if she can relieve her distress by taking time out to relax and nourish herself, then the time spent together will be more meaningful. With regular food, exercise, and sleep, she will be more present for the Son.

Help me. Help me, please. I need it.

March 16, 2010

3:18 p.m.

The Son's doctor calls with the test results. His numbers are slightly improved.

PART II

APRIL 15-JUNE 7, 2010

April 15, 2010

10:47 a.m.

The Mother remembers today that the Son is dying. Things have been different, since his nurse's most recent visit. His feet are cold. His complaints are weak. He is small and thin.

The vomiting has been under control, but now he has diarrhea.

She covers him with a fleece blanket. This navy blue blanket is printed with moons and stars. It is as if the universe were taking the Son into its arms.

The energy in the room has changed. There is a deep sense of stillness.

It may be almost time for him to go.

The Mother is crying, though not exactly for the Son. She knows that he will be alright. He will reappear somewhere, as something else—an angel, a seraph, a body of light. The Son will know the glory of the Father, of the eternal Spirit.

She cries more for herself, because his adorable presence will no longer be with her.

She loves the Son.

111

To share space with him and to care for him brings great joy.

In time, she will be alone.

The grieving has already begun.

1:06 p.m.

The Mother remembers that her great-aunt used to say, *You've got to get on with it.* This was her advice, whenever the Mother was upset.

The Mother doesn't think that her great-aunt meant we should deny, suppress, or forget about what is happening. She may have meant to accept the loss and continue.

There is a difference between getting over something and getting through it.

To move through loss is to acknowledge the loss and give ourselves time to grieve. We open to the situation as it is. We remove the smiling mask of denial and allow sadness to arise. It is natural to grieve when someone we love leaves us or dies.

In deepening our experience, we learn to be present with the sorrow. We don't fight against it. We don't struggle with a loss that is beyond our control.

Nor do we judge ourselves for the sadness we feel.

Instead, we attend to the grief with tender attention. In this way, the secondary suffering around our sorrow can be relieved.

We relax with grief. We give ourselves ample time and space to cope with the loss, to integrate it fully into the stream of our lives.

So, the intensity of our sorrow becomes such that we can breathe and continue.

Loss can be poignant rather than devastating, when we experience it in the full context of our rich emotional lives.

How interesting that we can feel more than one emotion at a time. We can hold both grief and love in the expansive heart. We can be patient with anger. We can face the fear of being left alone, in a space of safety. We can rediscover joy, in the midst of an unpredictable world.

3:26 p.m.

The Son's nurse has been using the word "palliative" lately. She has been through this before, with a grandparent, a parent, or perhaps even a sibling.

She says that the treatment is just keeping the Son from declining further.

She is realistic about his prognosis. She, too, is beginning to grieve in anticipation of the loss. Even as a medical professional, she will miss him.

She and the Mother discuss the emotional and spiritual aspects of his treatment. They think about how to keep him comfortable, when medical care can do no more.

The Mother will hold him.

The Mother will sing to him.

The Mother will pray with him.

And how will the Mother handle the situation?

She will remain open and curious.

She will not project catastrophe for the future. She will stay present.

What will it be like when he dies? We don't know.

His nurse reassures the Mother, letting her know that she is available whenever she or the Son need her, both in person and by telephone.

The Mother thanks her.

The Mother and his nurse pray for the strength, courage, and wisdom to care for the Son, so that he can transition peacefully, when the time is right.

They may be of different religions. They have never discussed their upbringings. This doesn't matter. They commune through their love for the Son.

8:49 p.m.

The Mother kneels at the window, before the open sky. She gazes up into the night.

She is grateful for the Son's presence here, this evening. She is grateful for his nurse's support. She gives thanks and surrenders the situation. She takes refuge in the Lord, from whence all arises and to whom all must return.

April 16, 2010

9:54a.m.

The vomiting and diarrhea are worse. They are becoming routine.

The Son's physical condition doesn't seem to bother him, however. He no longer complains or even mentions it. He takes his symptoms in stride.

The vomiting happens, and then it's over.

In the Mother's mind, a feeling of helplessness arises.

Even when they aren't in the same room, she aware that he is here, lounging on the sofa, taking in the sunshine.

He is present while she reads, writes, paints, cooks, and prays.

He is gentle and kind. Still, he will leave her, through no wish of his own.

1:17p.m.

The Mother learns from the Son.

He is very sick, and there is nothing more that medical treatment can do. Still, he is gentle and patient.

I don't know if I will be able to stand watching him suffer at the moment of death.

Then, she remembers.

She will not be aloof to his suffering. She will be holding him.

Maybe she will not sing or pray.

Maybe, she will cry.

Maybe they will listen together to the sound of tears that fall like spring rain.

3:14p.m.

To discontinue treatment at this point seems like a mixed blessing. There would be no more doctor's visits. There would be no more needles and no more disappointments—no more finding out that his weight has dropped again or that his blood levels are up. No more of that.

On the other hand, his nurse is a source of support for both of them. She visits regularly. She is unhurried. She listens to the Mother's concerns about the Son's condition. If the Son were to ask questions about his condition or treatment, she would answer them.

His nurse is strong. She cares about them both. The Mother knows that his doctor does, too.

April 17, 2010

10:30a.m.

The Son's doctor calls this morning. The lab has run his tests stat. This bloodwork is of high priority.

His doctor tells the Mother that the Son's numbers have improved. The vomiting and diarrhea will most likely calm down on their own.

April 26, 2010

2:35p.m.

What can we do?
Something magnificent,
or nothing at all.
The master knows that
there is no difference.

The Son's illness overwhelms the Mother.

Why should this be so, when his test results are
improved?

She considers the situation further.

Why, if his numbers are better is he still so
symptomatic? Why is there nothing that anyone can
do to relieve his suffering?

5:14p.m.

The Mother thinks of the way her life has
changed, since the Son's arrival several months
ago. For so many years, she has lived contentedly
without him. Now, she cannot imagine her life
without him in it.

Someone once imagined that an event so simple as a butterfly flapping her wings might, as one thing leads to another, affect weather patterns across the oceans. This phenomenon, this simple variation in initial conditions, is referred to as the Butterfly Effect.

A simple action, like the Son's arrival, affects the world.

The Butterfly Effect is a part of the Chaos Theory.

We create theories out of chaos, to find some sense of order.

Chaos Theory explains that, although we think that we can determine an outcome based on expected cause and effect, the slightest variation in initial conditions may lead to unpredictably divergent results. This, then, is the Butterfly Effect. We cannot predict what we think we can predict.

The slightest adjustment we make in our life, or in becoming a part of someone else's life, may have an unexpected and far-reaching effect over time.

So, we find meaning in simple, daily actions, in a loss that we cannot understand.

April 25, 2010

10:46a.m.

The Mother sits at the window with her breakfast cereal. She looks out through the glass at the rising brick wall of the apartment building across the courtyard.

Beside her stands a solitary bamboo tree.

It is lean and graceful.

At one time, two stalks grew from the pot, but one of the cats has chewed and batted at the plant. Now there is only one.

This bamboo tree is alone, as I will soon be.

Boil water for tea,
toast sliced bread,
wash and fold sheets,
sweep away dust.
Then, sit quietly.
Listen,
a little boy
with a round pot
belly, somewhere
across the waters,
still waits to be fed.

10:57a.m.

I should be
someone else, I think,
someone who is
something more,
someone who is
anyone
but who
I am,
for who am I?

4:57p.m.

The riverbanks
are grassy.
They are not a meadow,
but they are grassy,
fragrant and green.

This earth could hold
any river.
Moss grows
over the roots of the trees,
strong and venerable,

GRIEF

one just like another,
like another.
Together they shade
the rich, black earth
that is here a river bank.
Earth bares herself
in soft streaks
for the waters.
Here, earth is as fragrant as grass.

April 30, 2010

7:16p.m.

"Mother,
how I wish I belonged to you," I say.
You think of me and
I am comforted,
as if the bold world
that I have taken on,
is being held in your gentle hands.
My heart remembers to sing.

"I would return home," I say,
but you remind me
that I left
years long gone.
It was not enough
to sit at your feet,
to gaze up at your face,
radiant purple bloom,
to share
unspoken secrets——

"Mother," I said,
"I cannot stay,

125

for there is much to be done,
so many tears to wipe
and brows to soothe,
so many hungry to be fed."

So, you have blessed me
with this life
apart from you
yet still,
so still
in the light.

8:09p.m.

Mother,
You are the great
empress
robed,
enthroned,
to receive
the sorrowful,
we who are confused,
we who are sick
with love for what
we do not know.

Mother,
all colors are in you.
Dark beauty,
sometimes you pull
your hair back—
severely.
I know you only
when the tendrils
play again
around your full moon face.

Mother,
sometimes you are
one with the sky;
there is
no beginning or end to you.
At times
you are radiant,
so radiant
that I need
to turn
into myself.

May 2, 2010

11:07 a.m.

The Mother prepares herself for the Son's departure.

Soon, I will be alone, again.

She realizes that even in our solitude, none of us lives alone. What we do affects others.

A butterfly in Thailand may be the cause of the breeze that blows in through the window, here.

Perhaps, here in New York City, the Mother is like a butterfly gently flapping beautiful wings.

She begins to see beyond her personal sorrow. She is an integrated part of the world. In caring for the Son, she participates wholeheartedly. His dying is part of a vastly bigger map of life.

May 3, 2010

5:17p.m.

When the Mother arrives on the detox ward, the day room smells like urine.

She mentions this jokingly to the occupational therapist.

He says that it's been one of those days.

She chats with one of the counselors, who is standing in the doorway of the small office.

Her cousin has stabilized and now wants to help others recover. He will start the training program to become an addiction counselor in September, at a college that is close to home.

"Recovery isn't something that you can buy," his mother, her aunt, says. "It is a gift that is given."

The occupational therapist rounds up the group.

The janitor begins to mop the floor with disinfectant. He is as important as anyone on the ward, in this simple work.

The Mother hands out new meditation worksheets.

The janitor slowly rolls the soaked mop and yellow plastic tub of now-dirty water out the door.

The group explores how our inner experience affects our lives.

Contentment doesn't arise simply from doing the right thing.

We want to be kind. We want to be useful. We want to fulfill our purpose in this life. That said, if things aren't right on the inside, nothing will feel right on the outside.

We need to make peace with ourselves to be at peace with our lives.

Sitting in meditation on the detox ward today, the Mother makes peace with the Son's dying.

She accepts that he will soon be gone, even as she will continue to do all that she can for him. Such is the surrender of our simple actions—to serve someone who is dying, without expectation. We hold the sorrow and the suffering, as we share loving presence.

When the Son passes, the Mother will grieve. She grieves already. This is a natural part of the dying process, for the Mother and for the Son.

They are opening. They are opening into the light.

9:27p.m.

The presence is the teacher.

The mind is the disciple.

What we need to continue growing can change over the years.

Though the mind may resist change, it is through change that we may find an even deeper peace, a stronger connection to the Lord.

May 5, 2010

4:59p.m.

We run,
run away,
though there's no need
to let the mind
chase us.
We can arrive
nowhere
but here.

5:11p.m.

We close the mind
around feeling,
like a fist
that holds
smoldering
coal,
so that everything
we touch then
burns with a fury.

May 6, 2010

12:05p.m.

The Son is dying.

The Mother cannot deny what is happening.

When he is gone, there will be things that she will wish she could share with him, like poetry.

She reads to him today, and he smiles. His quiet smile brings joy.

The Mother discovers in herself fresh pain, pain that has been too deep to feel, pain that has been numbed by denial, fantasy, and even the trappings of spirituality.

Feeling safe enough and strong enough to know our pain means that we are healing.

So, the emotional mind dissolves into light.

GRIEF

May 7, 2010

2:32p.m.

Just sit.
Sit in the light
of the shrine
within.

She who sits
within the shrine
is everything
and no one.

If praise words were
cried aloud
they would echo
in her dreams,
in her blessed inner visions,
for she has abandoned herself
to truth.

She may dance.
She may cry out
in the ecstasy

of song.
You will never know,
unless you too
can sit
in the clear light
that illuminates all
that is all that
has ever
or will ever be
and that, too,
which is never
to be known.

I bow to my the Lord
and ask only,
"Make me
yours, and yours
alone."

3:07p.m.

Do I have the courage
to give up everything
for the love of you?

135

5:42p.m.

The path is not about being good.
Am I?
The path is more than this. To live truly is about being one with all that is.

5:59p.m.

The individual feels an urge to be a part of something, to be included, to have a place, to play a distinctive role.

Awakening, however, is about being absorbed into the source of all.

7:14p.m.

What is there
for me
to do?
All is
as it should be—
taken care of.
You are the thousand
hands, feet,
eyes, mouths,

faces of the
universe.

I would stand up
and shout
"I shall save the world,"
but I cannot,
for it has already
been done.

I am free.
I am free.
I am free.

May 9, 2010

1:15p.m.

The Mother's mother comes over to visit the Son. The Mother welcomes her to visit.

The three of them sit together.

Relationship can be difficult, as well as illuminating.

Daily interactions are like experiments in the lab of consciousness.

How can I interact so that things will be most harmonious for me and my loved ones?

How can I respond, so that I will feel good about my behavior and whatever happens next?

We ask ourselves these questions.

We need not take each turn of events so personally.

One day, we awaken to find ourselves living without being disappointed or hurt. We feel a steady sense of tranquility, as circumstance unfolds.

May 11, 2010

9:42a.m.

The Mother sits at the Son's bedside, which has become like an altar, and writes in her journal.

10:25a.m.

Why sit silent at the shrine?

Lie on your back in the grass
on the first spring morning,
early, before anyone
else discovers
that strawberries grow wild
in the dirt.

You could tend to them,
gently trowelling weeds,
watering
from a greening copper can,
while a bird warbles
somewhere in the branches
of the nearby

139

GRIEF

tangerine tree.
You could harvest
too many tangerines
for your hands
to hold,
lemons,
nectarines,
sweet with
the sun's heat,
a weathered basket
full of blue plums,
and a handful of
anonymously pretty
flowers for the
window sill.

You could, but
you don't.

You lie there in the grass,
arms outstretched,
and the bird
continues to sing.

11:03a.m.

The morning
glory
opens full-faced
to the sun.
At night,
she's elusive,
more elusive
than her
soft fragrance,
more elusive yet
than your
most intimate
breath.

11:09a.m.

This body
of supple clay
is to be known
only with tenderness.
You could be touched,
and you are.

You feel the light change.
You become the sky.

8:57p.m.

Assume
with a full heart
that all mean well.
Rejoice.
Be free.

9:01p.m.

Action
invites reaction
to become new
action.

It's not personal—
so don't react.

If you want to be free,
be free.

9:07p.m.

Attach not to
what you do,
to what another
does.
Let mind be
clear of intention.
In the open space
of play,
you are free.
You are free
in this mind-blowing
world
and beyond.

9:15p.m.

Love light
completely,
and light
will not be able
to get enough
of you,
playing along
the curves,

tickling
every crevice
of mind,
expanding to fill
your very being
until you don't know
anymore
who you
ever were.

9:15p.m.

The Mother is preparing for an upcoming teaching with the primordial *lama,* the golden Buddha of Compassion.

She studies the *Bodhisattvacaryavatara*.

Here, Shantideva describes the value of staying alert to virtue.

All deeds are directed towards joy,
upon which no price
can be placed.
Rejoice in the virtue
of others' deeds.
So, experience that joy.   5.77

Rather than finding fault with others, laying blame, or angering, we take joy in virtue.

We encourage virtue by noticing virtue.

We walk a peaceful path in appreciating the virtue in those around us.

We nourish the seed of enlightenment.

We bow down with body, speech, and mind.

Whoever is before us, we may delight, with a smile, a joke, or a compliment, with a helping hand, with a small gift.

We are delighted by this being.

When we care enough for this being, as for any being, to look into this truth, we are amazed at the endless wealth of benevolence that we discover. Hidden treasure is brought suddenly to light.

May 13, 2010

9:30a.m.

The Mother contemplates the virtue of patience.

She has a choice—to worry over the Son's dying or to release anxiety into patience.

Patience is in not found in expecting immediate healing.

True patience may be to expect nothing from our discipline, our service, our sacrifice. True patience may be as simple as taking joy in what we do each day.

4:47p.m.

The Son has eaten very little for nearly three days.

He looks skeletal.

No. It's not that bad.

The Mother's mind is exaggerating. Emotion brings delusion—the fear, the angst.

She doesn't want to lose him, though she knows well that she will.

May 14, 2010

7:16p.m.

The Son looks into the Mother's eyes, and she feels it in her soul.

She is satisfied that he knows the Lord.

He lays his head against her shoulder, and she feels at peace.

May 15, 2010

8:30a.m.

The Son does not want to eat breakfast this morning, though he does drink his usual cup of green tea.

If he is leaving, it means that he has finished what he was to do here. He has experienced all that he needed to experience in this lifetime. He has fulfilled his duty in this particular adorable form.

May 16, 2010

11:06a.m.

Each face is a flower—
the inquisitive
rose,
full-blown
peony, or
wide-eyed
pansy,
the fragrant lily,
unabashed
sunflower,
playful daisy,
or whispering
heather
field grown wild,
into the open sky.

12:32p.m.

The Mother considers that the death of a loved one, this unavoidable circumstance, may be a different experience for each of us.

Our response will depend upon our relationship to death. How did we first experience death? Has dying been a taboo subject in our household, or is it openly accepted as a part of life? Have we made peace with our own mortality?

Experience depends upon our willingness to be with what is. In saying *yes* to transformation, we become receptive to the divine grace that carries us into the light.

2:37p.m.

Do not resist
the call to turn
now
and face the truth.
It has always
been in you.

7:00p.m.

The Mother volunteers on Sunday evenings at a homeless shelter.

Still, she does not like to leave the Son, alone.

She sets him up with a small reading lamp and a stack of good books.

He shoos her away, playfully.

She kisses his cheek, on her way out the door.

The shelter is housed in a church basement. In the distance, a security guard whistles, as he strolls the length of the hallways.

Someone has left dinner to be heated in a covered aluminum tray on the kitchen counter. Another volunteer takes care of the food. The Mother handles the paper plates, the plastic pitcher of ice water, and a ceramic bowl full of green grapes.

She distributes blankets, sheets, and towels. One folded set is placed at the foot of each cot.

Tonight, the shelter is short a few towels. Some of the women will not be able to shower.

The women arrive with a clatter of footsteps and cheerful greetings. They sign in on the triplicate form, choose their cot for the evening, and lay aside their overnight satchels.

Some push the cots close together, seeking companionship.

Others find a space by themselves, for they have been waiting in lines or sitting in loud crowded rooms, all day.

They will stay overnight in this expansive cavern, with its arched wooden doorways and green-painted pillars.

Together, they enjoy lasagna and a loaf of day-old bread. They share the details of the day—the job search, drug rehab, church steps.

To be here with these women is fulfilling.

When the Mother returns home, she and the Son discuss the shelter's shortage of towels, the requests for more vegetables, and the grief that the women experience in their loss of home, family, and dignity.

The Son wonders whether they might shelter women here, along with the once-abandoned cats.

May 17, 2010

7:42p.m.

The Son rests. He is pale and thin. He has pulled the covers up around his neck for warmth.

The Mother sits beside him, on a flowering carpet, with a book in her lap.

Shantideva teaches on emptiness as an antidote to grief, in the *Bodhisattvacaryavatara*.

> *If a dream child dies,*
> *understanding that*
> *the child has never existed*
> *but for the temporary matrix*
> *of cause and condition*
> *assuages sorrow,*
> *even as the child*
> *neither exists*
> *nor ceases to exist.*   *9.140*

8:47p.m.

A seed alone
remains no more
than seed, dry.
Tamp it deep
into earth,
let water flow,
let the sun continue
to rise and to set,
for so a seed sprouts.

The mango tree
fruits quietly.
A flowering vine
drives the night
with her soft call.
These are seed songs.

8:59p.m.

The Mother meditates on the Son's bamboo chair. Its straw seat is plain and fragrant.

He has chosen this chair over a painted bench that is padded with blankets, and even a comfortably upholstered armchair.

When he is not coloring at her desk, he is to be found in bed or in this chair.

A bamboo tree
may one day
become
your cane chair,
and so will you be held
by the earth,
the rain,
the fragrance of jasmine,
ripe fruit,
the sun's light,
on boughs
that have been
uprooted,
dried
and tenderly bent.

9:07p.m.

Compassion
is as fire

unto gold,
releasing dross
alloy into the heat.

9:18p.m.

This dying child lives
in the way I
boil beans,
and quietly
sweep the floor.
So will he live
in each ordinary day,
because I have done
these things for him.
There is sweetness
in grief.
Tears will be
a new kind of laughter.
I take joy
in having known
him, in knowing
him still
in the beans I boil,
in the floor I sweep,
in the new tenderness

that I hear in the wind's voice.
It breathes
everywhere.

8:36p.m.

Mourn one who moves on
as if he were the hollow
sound of wind in trees.

157

May 18, 2010

8:06a.m.

The Son plays at eating his breakfast. The solitary morsels of toast he crunches are nothing compared to what he usually eats, but he eats.

The Mother makes a conscious effort not to focus on each mouthful he takes, or doesn't. She opens to the whole room, as she sits at the table beside him.

The kitchen countertop has been scrubbed clean. The refrigerator stands and hums. It is stocked with nourishing, organic produce. Through a distant doorway, her desk is stacked with books and files.

There is more to my life than what he eats.

There is more to the lives of people in this world than one small breakfast of toast and green tea.

She tries not to worry.

She simply notices that he eats, or that he doesn't.

She eats.

She takes refuge in the gentle breath.

She abides in the joy that he is sitting across the table from her, perpetually amazed.

9:16a.m.

A friend telephones to ask how the Mother is doing, how he is doing.

They sit together, on the telephone. The Mother is on the floor beside a bookcase. Her friend is calling from her artist's loft, where gargantuan painted flowers lean up against the walls.

The Mother tells her friend that the Son is dying, that her sorrow is deep.

How much longer will he be here? Nobody knows. This is a part of the struggle, not knowing.

The friend offers kind wisdom.

We sit with *I don't know*. The "I" dissolves into space.

So, we open into *Don't Know*.

11:42a.m.

The Mother will remain a tender witness. She will support him through these transformations.

Today, she doesn't want to act strong or stoic.

GRIEF

She will just be as she is, today—vulnerable
to change, tender of heart.

May 20, 2010

2:47p.m.

The Mother asks the Son about his lack of appetite, about his nausea. Indeed, he feels too sick to eat. He agrees to go to see his doctor.

The Son does not wear a jacket for the simple walk to his doctor's office. His fair skin is luminous. He looks unearthly, as if he were visiting from another realm.

Soon, he will be passing on.

His doctor enters the examining room and closes the door. The Mother is so relieved to see her that she almost starts to cry.

This doctor is motherly, though she may be as youthful as the Mother. It would probably be alright with his doctor if the Mother did cry. His doctor would comfort her.

But there is no need to cry.

His doctor starts telling the Mother and the Son that everything is okay. She gives the Son a thorough examination. There are different possibilities and various options to explore. Maybe they need to raise his dose of fluids. An appetite stimulant might help. Perhaps the problem is his teeth——one of them is abscessed. Varying his diet might help.

In the stark examining room with its cold steel table, the three of them stay open to the potential for improvement in the Son's condition.

They will know more tomorrow, when they receive the results of his blood tests.

7:32p.m.

The Mother cooks, while the Son rests.

The kitchen countertop becomes a buffet of delights, soups——steamed beans, and fresh bread.

The Son pushes the plates away, though the food is very fresh and hot, the way he likes it.

He would eat, but he cannot.

He wants to go to bed, early.

Tonight, he will not stay up making mischief, long after the lights are out.

Sometimes, the Mother scolds him playfully, hugging him in the darkened temple and telling him to get back into bed.

Not tonight. He is tired.

May 21, 2010

3:35p.m.

The Son's doctor calls with the results of the blood tests. His numbers are not good.

Standing in the back office with the telephone receiver in hand, the Mother's first impulse is to pray for a miracle.

Does anyone not pray that their loved one recover?

Consider this prayer. We are asking for a change in the natural order of things, as a special dispensation. We are asking that our loved one be the only one never to die.

Instead, the Mother sits down before a large window in the temple. She prays for the Lord's will to be fulfilled.

The Son has brought such love into so many lives.

Even his nurse has been transformed. She has always been strong and cheerful. Now, she is noticeably gentle.

She is tender with him, as she kneels down to look into his eyes and ask how he is feeling, this afternoon.

4:01p.m.

The Mother holds the Son. A broad and pale freckle the spreads across the inside of his right ear. This freckle is one of the things that the Mother finds most endearing about him.

Grief is natural.

The tears do come, but she feels a sense of strength. She loves him. This love is stronger than sadness.

The Son grows more peaceful with each passing day. He is happy and comfortable.

4:33p.m.

The Son is a gentle and pure soul.

He would not make a notable fiction character, for he has no edge. He is unconflicted. He is straightforward and kind.

The Mother recalls an ancient Indian hymn about the sweetness of the Lord.

The Lord is nothing but sweetness—*madhura*. How sweet are his glance, his laugh, and his saunter. How sweet are his wanderings and even his absence.

The Son is sweet like this, and so will be his absence.

5:53p.m.

The Mother contemplates the story of Kisa Gotami, the young mother who in grieving for her dead child visits the Buddha, accepts the impermanence of creation, and renounces the world to awaken.

How does grief bring enlightenment, like a flash of lightning in the dark of night?

When we understand that sorrow is a part of everyone's experience, we devote ourselves to seeking liberation from this sorrow, for the welfare of all beings. Life may be as simple as this.

The path is one of gentle and steady practice. We serve with a pure heart, until one day, we too will awaken from the dream of sorrows. Yes, as certain for each of us as is death is enlightenment.

May 22, 2010

9:57a.m.

Early blue light falls across the window. The bamboo plant that grows beside a solid bookcase is brilliantly green in this light.

The Mother takes refuge in the morning chores.

She chops vegetables for the day's meals.

She folds laundered sheets, neatly. They are still warm from the dryer and smell of lavender.

The sunrise is gentle.

The sky has turned to rose.

The Son eats a good breakfast.

2:30p.m.

The Mother speaks with his doctor about their options. Sedation. Hospitalization. Raw suffering.

With good intention, none of these would be wrong. None of them feels right, either.

There may be no right answer.

This is a relief.

They will take things as they come. They will do the best they can with whatever arises.

The Son is weakening and visibly sick.

The Mother prays quietly.

May 23, 2010

8:45p.m.

The Son is lively, today.

The Mother takes his renewed spunk in stride. There will be ups and downs.

Today, he eats more than he has in the past two days, and he enjoys his meals.

His appetite seems to be steadily increasing.

He is very hungry for dinner and eats a more than he has all day—almost half a plate of food.

The Mother cooks for him with abandon. She chops, steams, and sautés at his request.

She feels satisfied.

May 24, 2010

8:14p.m.

The Mother walks home from the hospital, where she has offered the usual meditation workshop.

There are no storefronts on this quiet street, just a block over from the river, where the sun blazes above still waters. The sunset does not go unnoticed.

Illuminated, the buildings are stately, some with polished brass trim, and others simpler in their dignity.

Lounging in doorways, the doormen wear smart caps and friendly smiles. They nod and wave.

The Mother breathes in the softening summer air. She enjoys this stroll.

More than a mile stretches ahead of her. She gazes into the vast expanse of evening. Is there any jewel so radiant as the night sky?

May 25, 2010

2:36p.m.

Identity—
tug it
this way
and that.
Try to drape
it just right.
Still, there is
clinging.

What is it like
to walk bare
and brazen?

4:03p.m.

Your call sounds
out into the starless dark
of not knowing,
of still wanting.
I have answered you,
before.
I have—

thinking,
yes, this is it.
I am sexless.
I am selfless.
I more or less
yours. I am.

4:32p.m.

Vows are
the first mossed
stepping stone,
the bridge mouth,
from material
world into light,
a light that is
insistent,
demanding,
wanting
all of you
now and now,
again.

4:47p.m.

If you think
you have,
you have not
lost your mind
to light.

5:07p.m.

In the clear light,
I am touching nothing.

8:15p.m.

The Mother has never been able to spend time with someone who is dying, like this.

She thinks back to her grandfather's death, to her great-aunt's death. They were shocking and sudden as the earthquakes that shook the floors when she was a child growing up in Los Angeles.

To know that the Son is dying and to have time to explore the grief, while he is still here, is a gift.

It is as if the Lord has invited them both to a party and given them each other to unwrap.

The Mother offers a silent prayer of gratitude.

She feels blessed to be present with him for the slow winding down, to know that death is coming, as death comes to us all, and to be at peace with it.

Death is a simple exhale.

Life is about transformation.

May 31, 2010

11:04p.m.

Watch oak leaves blowing
in hot summer wind. There's no
thing left to desire.

1:17p.m.

Seated on the floor, the Son is making a collage out of brown parcel paper. He does not use outlines or scissors. Instead, he tears the pieces of paper freehand, to create silhouettes of animal images—a cat, a fish.

He carefully adds detail, like the definite stripe he tears across the top of the paper cat's head.

This is a portrait of one of the rescue cats, who does indeed have a white face and blazed forehead.

The Son works quietly beside boxed back issues of the literary magazine.

He hums to himself, little ditties that he creates along with the paper animals.

The Mother edits the new issue of the magazine at her desk.

His gentle voice resounds in her heart.

4:15p.m.

The Son rests with the window wide open. Beyond its painted frame, the foliage is lush with humidity.

A small but powerful fan hums in the hot room.

The Mother sits at the Son's bedside.

Children are being born in the hospital where she teaches, just blocks away. The possibilities of life are endless, even as he lies here dying.

This is the cycle of change. As things fall away, so new life arises.

The Mother tells the Son that she loves him.

He smiles, quietly.

The sky's luminescence is within him.

4:47p.m.

The large golden tabby is the Son's favorite of the rescue cats that they care for. This big fellow likes to drink from the bathtub faucet.

Now, he meows from the bathroom.

The Mother turns the tap, so that the water runs in a thin stream, so that the tabby can suckle without getting drenched. The cat may still miss his mother from whom he was weaned too early.

The golden tabby is large enough to be a lion cub. He lowers his noble head to lap up the water that splashes into the tub.

"Drink from the source," the Mother tells the golden tabby. "That way, what you take in is pure."

Once the water has flowed into the tub, it picks up all kinds of things—tile cleaner, scented soap, hydrating shampoo.

The Son watches him eagerly, from the doorway.

To drink from the faucet is like seeking the Lord directly, holding nothing back.

The Mother points the cat gently back up to the faucet.

"Drink from the source."
It is what she would say to anyone.

June 2, 2010

2:31p.m.

One day soon, he will
be gone, like a long soft sigh
in the wind beyond.

June 4, 2010

7:14p.m.

Bright twilight, bamboo,
a window——I have never seen
blue like this before.

8:32p.m.

Sometimes, the Mother thinks that the Son has drawn his last breath. She leans in to check for the almost imperceptible rising and falling of his chest.

Hours later, he surprises her. Out of nowhere, he's hungry again. He's walking without stumbling. He's alert, and even vibrant. Yes, vibrant is a good word to describe him in these last few days of a life well-lived.

He will carry with him memories of crazy school days and the tenderness of loved ones. Or perhaps, he will dissolve into light.

June 5, 2010

4:16p.m.

Along the path, some
walk, some run. Lilies stand still,
in the tall green grass.

5:53p.m.

The Son's eyes are clear and distant, as if he were staring off into some faraway land.

The Mother wonders whether he sees where he will be going, whether there are wise ancestors, trumpeting angels and heavenly clouds, or just a vision of love far greater than anything that we could ever long for here in this world.

When he does speak, his voice is strong and musical.

He wants no funeral. There is no need for people to stand around his stiff boxed form to memorialize him. He would rather be remembered as living, or realized as light.

She should not spend her time on morbid arrangements but live with a joyful heart.

June 6, 2010

8:40a.m.

The morning duties are a meditation.

The Mother slices an apricot for the breakfast cereal. She notices the fine and subtle color of the fruit, its imperfect roundness, the almost imperceptible touch of its skin against her fingers.

The room is bright.

The laundry is fresh.

The Mother washes the Son, as well.

She is trying to keep his mouth clean, so that he will be more comfortable. He has an oozing sore, an abscess in his upper right gums, and his right cheek is swollen.

He gazes at her with innocent eyes.

The day he dies will be a day like any other.

2:47p.m.

The Son can no longer walk.

Sometimes, he cries out, softly.

GRIEF

He likes the Mother to sit with him, and to hold his hand.

He is her beautiful boy.

June 7, 2010

10:42a.m.

The Mother feels uneasy.

What will happen when I go to teach meditation on the detox ward?

The Son's doctor has mentioned seizures as a possibility.

If I go out, I might not be here when he needs me.

He is watching a candle dance. The bright flame is fascinating.

I do not want him to die alone.

She clears the day.

She sits next to the Son, and reads silently from the *Svetasvatara Upanishad*. The verses do not need to be spoken aloud. He feels every word. The Mother is certain of this.

1:16p.m.

He eats nothing today. His eyes are distant.

Still, he is gentle, loving, and contented. His voice is stronger.

He tells the Mother that he feels fine and not to worry.

He is joyful, though his body is finished.

3:19p.m.

The Mother thinks of homes for the dying, of nuns who carry forgotten outcasts in stretchers from the streets of India, so that they may die in loving dignity.

What can I do to make him comfortable?

She need not sit here, helplessly. She is a competent caretaker, and she loves him.

She dampens a cloth with warm water and begins to wash his face. She cleans all around his lips, and the sore inside. She cleans his mouth gently, for a long time.

He sips at a cup of water that she holds for him.

Then, they both sit back.

He tells her again that he is not suffering, that he is happy.

4:03p.m.

She is lying next to him when he dies. He wants it to be like this.

Her arm is around him. His hand is on her cheek.

This gesture surprises her. He has never been affectionate in quite this way, before. His eyes are locked on hers.

She cries softly, because she knows that he is leaving. She cries for him, while he is still here, and he comforts her, with his hand on her cheek.

"I love you," she says.

An incredible peace settles. It is as if someone had hushed the room, so that they might focus completely on each other's eyes.

They lie together like this for a long time, maybe for hours.

The Mother remembers that a nurse is supposed to be coming over in the late afternoon, perhaps anytime now.

What if he is in the midst of dying, and she calls?

The Mother doesn't want to get up then, to answer the telephone or the door.

What if I don't answer and the bell keeps ringing?

It is not his usual nurse who will be coming, today.

Today is Monday. This is his nurse's day off. This is her day off, but she had wanted the Son to have extra care. She has asked a colleague to stop in, even though this is not a day when his usual treatment is scheduled.

The Mother takes her arm from around the Son and sits up to call the new nurse, to tell her not to come over, that they are doing fine as they are. Then, they will be able to rest like this all afternoon, without interruption.

She takes her arm from around him and sits up to make the phone call.

He cries out. It is finished.

His head goes back, and his teeth grind. He vomits.

The Mother puts her hand on his head and brings it forward, so that he is looking into her eyes, again.

"I'm here," she says. "I'm here."

She wipes away the vomit with the cloth she had used to wash his face, just hours ago.

Even now, he is surprised, pleased by her efficiency.

She lies down again and puts her arms around him.

He begins to take short sharp breaths. There are longer and longer spaces between them. Each time he breathes, they are not sure that there will be another.

And then, there is nothing.

He is not breathing. The Mother thinks that he has died.

Two days earlier, he stopped breathing. He stopped breathing for quite some time. The Mother thought that he had died.

And then, as suddenly, he began to breathe again.

When his nurse arrived that afternoon, the Mother cried in her arms.

His nurse visited them twice that day. She'd stopped by again in the evening, to listen to his heart, to bring him a present, to see him again.

Now suddenly, he takes in a sharp breath.

The Mother begins to pray the Rosary.

Hail Mary full of grace,
the Lord is with thee.
Blessed art thou among women,
and blessed is the fruit of thy womb, Jesus.
Holy Mary, Mother of God,
pray for us sinners,
now and at the hour of our death.

This is the moment of conversion.

Tears stream from her eyes.

She tells him that she loves him. She thanks him for being a part of her life.

She tells him, "I love you," over and over again.

He is looking into her eyes. They are breathing, together.

The space between breaths gets longer and longer, until there is not another one. The last breath is sweet and easeful.

His eyes dilate slowly.

She knows that he has died.

She wraps his body in her saffron robe.

PART III

JUNE 7-JULY 4, 2010

June 7, 2012

5:43p.m.

The new nurse does not call.

She simply arrives and makes arrangements for the lifeless form, now no longer him.

The Mother calls everyone who needs to know. She tells them. She tells them that his was a good death.

She leaves out the part about the seizure. She wishes that the seizure hadn't happened, and anyway, what good would it do anyone to suffer through its description.

She remembers that trained health care professionals will tell the patient what they are going to do before they do it. Perhaps she should have told the Son, no asked him, what he wanted to do about the nurse's visit at that moment, before removing her arm from around him.

Now, she tells their friends that she is happy.

She is happy. She is happy that he is no longer suffering, and that he died lovingly.

His last breath was peaceful.

6:39p.m.

She takes a short, slow walk around the neighboring reservoir. The waters are calm.

She returns home. He does not meet her at the door. Instead, grief socks her in the stomach.

She feels lonely, and she misses him terribly.

She cries out his name, loudly. Tears flow.

She doesn't know how she will make it through this first night without him.

8:06p.m.

The bag of fluids is still hanging from a hook on the bathroom door.

The needles are in a small box on a table in the living room.

The medicine dropper and the pills that the Mother used to crush up and dilute for him are still on the kitchen counter.

These things, at least, are still where they have always been, though he is not.

She wanders aimlessly through the empty rooms. She feels lost here, without him.

June 8, 2010

9:05 a.m.

When the Mother rose yesterday, the challenge was to face the Son's impending death.

Today, the new challenge is to face the day without him.

The golden tabby cat noses around the carton of his fluid bags, broken open on the floor by a bookcase in the sitting room.

This is difficult for all of them.

The Mother rises to comfort the cat. She holds him in her arms, as if he were the Son. She buries her face in his bronze stripes.

Love transforms us.

She is thankful to have been able to care for the Son, to have known such love.

9:12a.m.

The Son often sat in the bamboo chair by a window in the office. The woven straw seat would creak gently as he shifted. The sound was comforting.

Family and friends call to offer condolences. Receiving their sympathies is like fulfilling a duty. She wants simply to sit quietly and grieve.

As she answers each telephone call in the office, she continues to notice that he is not sitting in his chair. Perhaps, she need not use the modern cordless telephone in the office.

An old-fashioned red telephone sits on a trunk full of blankets in the sitting room. It reminds her of the telephones her family used when she was a child. This telephone is a line to a time before loss.

She realizes that she is saying goodbye not only to the Son, but also to his nurse, who lent structure to their days.

Sometime after lunch, the telephone would ring. At the other end of the line, his nurse would say that she was on her way.

Minutes later the doorbell would buzz, and her broad smile would greet them both.

For nearly six months now, the Mother has planned work meetings, walks in the park, grocery shopping, and trips to the pharmacy around these afternoon visits.

His nurse had visited twice the day before the Son had died.

During her usual afternoon visit, she had listened intently to his heart.

That evening, she had returned. She'd brought him a shimmering stuffed fish with green felt fins.

The Son's eyes had grown big and round upon receiving it, in the dim lamp light of his room.

He had been too amazed even to thank her, but she knew that he knew that she loved him.

He'd died the next day.

Now, his nurse is gone, too.

9:15a.m.

The Mother tries to remember what she had been working on, these past few days before he died. Whatever it was must still be stacked on the desk, where they would sit together.

Yes, she had been editing the new issue of the literary magazine. She had been developing a new workshop for the psychiatry patients. She had been studying a new old chapter of the *Bhagavad Gita*.

When somebody dies, he moves on to the next experience, whatever that may be.

We continue with what we are doing, here. The situation is simple. There is nothing difficult to figure out. This is not like those early weeks, when they were deciding what to do about the Son's treatment.

The Mother makes a mental note that she will continue with the work that she had been doing. She will pick up the friendships, meetings, and exercise that she had left aside.

She had not wanted to leave the Son for long. Now, she can go out for as long as she likes, whenever she likes. There is a new kind of freedom, for he is gone.

Still, this freedom is hollow.

His bamboo chair sits empty at the window.

10:52 a.m.

A friend calls to help with the literary magazine's website. He lives in Canada. He knows nothing of the Son.

The Mother and her friend talk about life, about not taking things personally, about doing things that are outside of our comfort zone, about building energy by loving our circumstances, about how this energy can elate others.

They reconstruct the magazine's website, filling it with features to make it more accessible, adding color, texture, and pictures.

Life continues to flow.

Another friend sends an e-mail reminding the Mother that their writing group will meet next week.

Life continues to flow.

The Son would want it this way.

He loved the Mother. He wanted her not to grieve but to be happy. He said as much before he died.

Still, she grieves.

Her life feels fragmented. She continues with what has been a satisfying life, but she cannot fully engage with the work to be done. There is little acknowledgment of this devastating loss, for the world around her continues as usual. What condolences she does receive feel empty. Her grief remains hidden, like a precious treasure of which the world around her knows nothing.

11:22a.m.

A large water beetle runs across the floorboards in the sitting room. The Mother calls the superintendent to please come upstairs and take care of it. He does so with ease, with his bare hands, without harming the beetle. He simply bends down, scoops it up, and carries it off to be set free.

The Mother decides to clean the rooms from stem to stern.

She gets down onto her hands and knees to scrub the kitchen floor.

She clears out two closets, emptying sundry unnecessaries into large plastic garbage bags, lightly scented with lemon.

She vacuums dust from the corners of the rooms, from beneath the chairs and bookcases.

There will be neither dust nor clutter when she has finished.

Cleaning the rooms thoroughly will not bring the Son back, but cleaning the rooms thoroughly gives the Mother something simple to engage with.

Little by little, she accomplishes the task.

She takes a bus downtown and brings home new curtains. They are sheer and white.

The linen drapes that have been hanging for years are dingy with dust.

The Mother is freshening up these rooms that feel empty without the Son.

She stands tall on a chair to hang the new curtains. They blow softly in the breeze, as if they are waving goodbye to him.

The Mother misses the Son.

The loss hurts. She has grieved and cried before, but she cannot remember loss ever hurting like this.

2:36p.m.

The Son's nurse arrives as usual, after lunch.

She is not here to give him the treatment, today. Today, she brings yellow daisies.

She says that yellow is his color. She says that the flowers are bright, like he is.

The Mother notices that she speaks of the Son in the present tense, as if he were still here. His nurse knows that the soul does not die.

The Mother tells her about the Son's death. As before, she leaves out the part about the seizure.

Why did I remove my arm from around him just at the moment of his death?

The Mother gives his nurse one of the last photographs she had taken of him. In the photograph, the Son is weak but pleased to pose. He sits tall, smiling wide-eyed into the camera.

The Mother remembers how he had turned playfully from one side to the other, so that she could find his best angle.

The Son's nurse begins to cry. She says that this picture is going into a frame right away. She asks the Mother to place the flowers in the Son's favorite spot.

Then, she too leaves.

The Mother is alone, again.

The Mother trims the stems of the yellow daisies in the kitchen, at an angle, under running water. To do so will make them last longer.

She arranges the flowers in a square vase. The glass catches the sunlight with its definite angles.

Which spot was his favorite?

The Mother places the daisies on his bamboo chair.

An hour or so later, she moves them to his bed.

Finally, she sets the flowers on the altar in the temple.

These flowers are a tangible symbol of his presence. They are bright, like he is.

Now, he is everywhere.

7:49 p.m.

The Mother steps out into the world that she knew before the Son's dying. She finds her way to the gym. She talks and laughs with a few friends there.

How strange not be aware of the time, not to think of his need, not to rush home to him.

The rooms are empty when she returns.

She chops ordinary vegetables for this evening's dinner and steams brown rice.

She peels and slices a tangerine for dessert. The sections fall apart into delicate and fragrant triangles. She spices them with coriander.

Then, she sweeps the pieces of orange from the wooden cutting board into a bowl that is painted with blossoms.

When the Son lay dying, the Mother cooked to calm herself, as well as to nourish him. She must have chopped so many pounds of vegetables and boiled gallons upon gallons of water to center herself, so that she could care for him in his illness.

She imagines potfuls of warm, sanctified water pouring down from the heavens to wash away the grief.

The loneliness in the kitchen is palpable, like the damp dishrag that sits crumpled at the side of the empty sink.

Even so, this night is easier than any night has been, since his death.

Tonight, the Mother can stand to turn out the lights when she goes to bed.

June 9, 2010

9:42 a.m.

The Son is on the Mother's mind as dawn breaks wide open.

In the new light, she tells him that she loves him.

She feels refreshed by a good night's sleep.

She rises to pray before the altar, in the breath of morning.

She sits on a cushion before the window, before the endless lightening sky. She gives thanks for their time together and prays for support and guidance.

10:30 a.m.

Upon entering the office, she finds that she is not ready to get back to work. The desk with its stacked papers, listed assignments, and gridded calendar are not what is needed, now. Timeline and due date overwhelm her.

She does not fight the grief.

She will be gentle with herself. She will allow time for the feelings to express themselves, for the tears to flow, for the soul to heal.

11:20 a.m.

The Mother sits at the window in his bamboo chair and reads from the *Svetasvatara Upanishad*. Its pages are pale and thin, as he was. She picks up where she had left off, on the day that he died.

> *Having performed worldly actions*
> *whosoever surrenders these deeds,*
> *as well as all intention behind them,*
> *is liberated from bondage to them.*   6.4

She has performed the caretaking actions. Now is the time to surrender them, to be freed from the bonds of sorrow.

She will continue to do what is to be done, without clinging to result. So, her soul will be purified, rather than bound, by action.

The commentary in the small purple volume refers to the *Bhagavad Gita*.

Whatever you do, do as an offering unto to me, says the Lord.

Whatever you do,
whatever you eat,
whatever you sacrifice,
whatever you give
whatever disciplines you practice,
do so as an offering to me.   9.27

Perhaps the Son has been offered unto the Lord as a blessed sacrifice. Yes, she is willing to offer him to the Lord, to the heavenly Father.

And now, what of the work to be done?

Whatever we do, we do to glorify the Lord.

So, we realize that we are a manifestation of that effulgent light in all. So, we are liberated.

The *Gita* verse is not just about clearing through work on a cluttered desk. The *sloka* details five kinds of action, through which we may come to know the Lord—self-care, charity, ritual, giving, and discipline.

Whatever you do,
whatever you eat,
whatever oblations you offer,
whatever you give away,

and whatever you give up,
all this, surrender to me.   *9.28*

The Mother contemplates the verse.

Do we make this offering to the glorious transcendence that is beyond the world, and even words?

Perhaps, the offering is made to the Lord in the being before us, to the dusty runaway who is homeless on the roadside, to the hospital patient who is temporarily separated from her faith community, to the prison inmate who may face more imminent danger locked in than he ever did on the streets. The Lord is in all and whatever is offered is offered unto the Lord.

We need only remain aware of the Lord's presence, in ourselves, in our loved ones, and beyond all this.

Even as we are side-tracked and confused again and again, we return to take refuge in the Lord, in the very heart of being.

12:06p.m.

The Mother loses herself in the park.

A light drizzle is falling. The day is pleasantly damp. It suits her mood.

She roams for a while, amongst the trees that stand in still gesture, like all shapes and sizes of man.

She rediscovers playfulness along the winding paths.

Breathing easily, she returns home.

When she walks through the door and into the lighted hallway, her first thought is that he is not here.

The pale walls are hushed.

The Son's absence pains her, even as she feels his imperceptible presence.

1:45p.m.

For lunch, she makes a spontaneous spring vegetable soup. She does not use a recipe but cleans and slices any fresh vegetable that she finds in the crisper.

> *Spring vegetable soup—*
> *crack brown eggs into the pot,*
> *and think of new life.*

GRIEF

2:19p.m.

I am in you.
You are in me.
The radiance—
almost unbearable.

2:26p.m.

I care for you
who fear
no intimacy.
In your need,
you don't turn away,
saying, "Stranger,
why do you come to me
like this?"

You remember,
breathing in the new light.
You remember that no time
has passed.
You remember
that we have never
been apart.

2:45p.m.

Caring for the Son has been the Mother's role for more than six months. Now that he is gone, she feels at loose ends, like frayed threads that dangle from a well-worn sleeve.

She cannot return to what was, for she has been transformed. She has been filled and then made empty, again.

3:06p.m.

I admit that in
those last few days, I never
thought he would soon die.

3:24p.m.

The Mother sits quietly with the flowers that the Son's nurse brought in his memory. She has placed them again on his bamboo chair.

These yellow daisies are a special to the Mother, because of what they meant to his nurse, because they reflect the Son's bright and wide-eyed presence.

4:00p.m.

The Mother feels the letdown of schooldays beginning after a lazy and humid summer. She is getting back to work, as usual. Perhaps she should stock up on boxes of new slim pencils and useful rubber erasers.

The season of her life has changed.

If the Son had moved away to a dusty town in the wine country or even an imaginary island across the ocean, she would feel this same loneliness. The difference now is that he will not return.

4:34p.m.

The experience now
is of what is not,
what is not
here,
of what is not here
anymore.

I walk into a room
and the first thing
I notice

is that he's not
sitting in the bamboo chair
at the writing desk
in front of the window
that overlooks oak trees.

I expect him to be here.
It has become unrecognized habit
to notice him first
when I walk into a room—
not the books stacked,
half-read and waiting,
not the still sitting telephone,
not the tubes of watercolor paint—
This experience now is
about negative space,
emptiness,
a void,
what's missing,
that ache,
the sweet pulling
apart.
This may be
transcendence.

9:06p.m.

This is really awful, the Mother thinks. Such a thought, while important to acknowledge, could lead to another and another, dragging her into deeper sorrow.

She chooses to shift the thought, gently.

These feelings of grief are normal.

I am strong enough to hold these feelings with a loving heart.

Grief is a common experience.

Even so, the experience is unique to each of us. We grieve in our own way and in our own time.

The Mother does not set a limit with the kitchen timer or the desk calendar. She trusts that the grief will eventually pass for her, as it has for all who have lost parents, siblings, lovers, friends, and children.

Somehow, the promise that the grief will pass brings both relief and concern. This experience of grief has become her new experience of the Son. She does not want to be disloyal to him. She does not want to forget him. She does not want to forget the love that they shared in the space of silent acceptance at the very end, which was one of the most intimate experiences that she has ever had.

No, the Son is not this grief. She can allow this grief to pass. She can grow in the love that they shared. Her heart will break open to an even deeper love.

She is glad that the Son did not want a funeral. She remembers being torn at her grandfather's funeral over whether or not to view his body. She was afraid of the corpse, afraid of death. Still, she could not bear to give up the chance to see her grandfather one last time. She feared that if she did not, she would regret the decision. So, she had viewed his body.

The man in the coffin was not her grandfather. He was not made-up, not garishly rouged as some are—unnatural. Still, he looked waxen, unreal.

This vision of the pale corpse imprinted itself upon her mind such that she found it difficult to remember her grandfather any other way.

Years later, she did not view her great-aunt's body. Even so, the grand funeral became for some time her predominant memory of their time together.

No. No belabored funeral for the Son.

The Son did not identify himself with the inert form that he had shucked off like a husk, or some kind of broken down vehicle.

He knew that he was Spirit.

Can I now take joy in the memories I hold of our time together, before he was sick?

What might it be like to find a new relationship with him as light?

The Mother thinks of him as the sun.

Walking along the river, as the golden orb sets low on the horizon, she walks with him.

Awakening in the morning to see light reflected on the window across the courtyard, she sees him.

At night, he sleeps somewhere beyond the moon. By day, he shines everywhere.

He is no longer in form, but he is with her. He is with everyone.

June 10, 2010

9:39a.m.

The Mother awakens to feelings of gratitude.

She is grateful to love the Son.

She will experience the grief, even as she begins again to appreciate the myriad blessings that are present, as her life continues.

She is ready to sit at her desk.

A small flower sits in a glass vase amongst the stacked books. This table is an altar. The work is the offering.

11:25a.m.

This morning, as the Mother reads from the *Svetasvatara Upanishad*, she translates.

> *There is no Lord in the world*
> *who is His Lord.*
> *No one commands Him,*
> *nor is there any sacred sign*
> *that can point to Him.*
> *He is the first cause that is uncaused.*

He is the Lord of the king
of the senses;
so He commands even mind,
intellect, and silence.
He knows no Creator.
No one reigns above Him.   *6.9*

2:45p.m.

Today is Thursday. Thursday is his nurse's day to visit. This is the first Thursday in many months that she has not been here.

The Mother notes this simple fact.

June 11, 2010

The Mother renews her intention to surround herself with loving people and to surrender herself to the Lord.

June 12, 2010

10:14a.m.

To live in love with the Lord, in love with life. This is the path that is before her, now.

12:42p.m.

Though grandfather clock tells truly
that the hour is late,
the light beyond the window
is of youthful afternoons.
Does the sun shine like this
only while spotted cows roam?

1:37p.m.

On the day the Son died, the Mother tucked his medicine dropper into a high corner of the linen closet.

Daily had she crushed and diluted his pills into juice, using this dropper to deliver the medicine, so that the edges of pill halves would not be rough his throat.

Days later now, she puts away the nurse's gift, the stuffed silver fish, the shimmering toy that made the Son's eyes grow round with wonder. This toy, too, had been placed in a favorite spot, on his bamboo chair.

Now, the Mother puts the plush fish away. She places it gently in the closet, beside his medicine dropper.

Grief rises like a flood.

1:54p.m.

Your touch so tender—
it brings me to tears. Only
then does breath come.

2:08p.m.

This life
is not about
making an impression
in the ever-shifting sands.
All is as it should be.
Play by the sea,
for you are needed,
as each one is—

219

wanted,
simply here,
a part of the whole
that would not be whole
without this breath,
however small,
however fleeting,
never meaningless.

2:17p.m.

You are the totem universe
with sun and moon for eyes,
a mind of sky.
Earth is your body.
I lie still upon it.
The streams are your
life force.
There is fire in your belly,
and I breathe.
We love without touching.
Am I in you, or
are you in me?
This is how it is with us.

2:55p.m.

Not like sunlight
is the light of fire—
fire in the wilderness,
fire in the stony hearth,
fire that needs stoking,
like pleasure
brief and unpredictable,
a constant need,
the impossible appetite
for gold, adoration,
and the stroking of skins.

3:07p.m.

I am the answer
to the sudden cry,
the last shuddering
breath,
the sigh of soft release,
the sudden and ecstatic light.

4:52p.m.

The Mother lies on the floor and stares up through a big window into the sky. She is able to relax, today.

She revels in youth, delights in freedom, and thanks the Lord for life.

June 13, 2010

1:42p.m.

The light within, so
like a first love. Pull me close—
I am lost in you.

1:56p.m.

As we think,
so we become,
so think
only of me.

2:03p.m.

The pain of being
torn
apart is poignant.
Angst passes,
a sigh in the wind.

2:11p.m.

I am
mother comfort,
fatherly benevolence,
protector,
friend,
the effortless laugh
on the brink
of desperately
imagined need.

3:37p.m.

Like the moon——
I may seem
to be not round
but half-full,
a mere sliver of light,
distant,
disappearing once again
into night.

Do you know that in full sun
I am bare, revealed
to be all that I am——

as more than I have
yet appeared to be.

Do you know
that in this
sweet turning
I have always been
complete?

4:02p.m.

Tell the story of creation.
Renew your holy vow
with no end,
to the sky.
Make sense of this troubled world,
of the sudden gift and jolt,
of disappearance.

Just breathe.

Touch my soul—
I dare you.

GRIEF

4:16p.m.

I am fleeting,
a cloud blown softly through sky,
nothing to hold onto.

4:20p.m.

This body is made
of the same stuff as diamond—

Know life to be tender,
though equally precious
as stone.

June 14, 2010

5:07p.m.

The Mother returns along city streets from the Harlem hospital where she has offered a meditation workshop.

She does not pick up his ashes, on the way home.

She passes a family dry cleaner and waves to the father who owns it.

She catches sight of her reflection in the windows of deli, drugstore, and flower mart.

She does not pick up his ashes.

She stops at the corner stand for a slice of pizza.

She and a friend once tried to determine what makes good pizza. It must be something about the sauce or the chewiness of crust, they decided.

This is good pizza. Today, she has no one to share it with.

She does not pick up his ashes.

June 16, 2010

4:45p.m.

Again, the Mother does not pick up his ashes.

They are dust, not him.

He had said as much, himself, when he asked for no funeral.

She misses his small serious face, his hair mussed from sleep, his silly freckles, and the abandon with which he loved life.

So sick, he had needed constant caretaking.

Her time is free, now.

The days stretch endlessly, vast and empty, like the way her gut feels without him here.

June 17, 2010

3:09p.m.

He has returned to me as ash
ash contained in an oblong box,
a box surprisingly attractive,
well-made of wood,
not painted tin but a box
of fine grained oak,
the corners rounded.

This box fits him,
though what it holds
is not who he was.
Would it be vague
to describe him as pure
and gentle?

I listen for his voice
in the sound of young leaves.

5:20p.m.

The Mother rolls down a green slope in the park, the way she did when she was four years old.

Then, the slope had been covered with snow and sledders. She had been red-jacketed with a small friend who wore glasses that made her look wise.

Today, the hillside is fragrant with clovery grasses. Letting go at the top is as much fun as it ever was.

The Mother laughs and laughs as the scenery keeps turning upside down. This tumbling makes it impossible for the mind to hold onto any view. So, the mind opens and releases into pure joy.

The Mother sits up in the grass and examines the clover. She is searching for a lucky four-leafer.

Instead, her fingers run across a leaf that is dried, fallen.

When a leaf falls, do the others mourn the loss of a brother?

She leans against the tree trunk. Its bark is rough, peeling.

This tree can hold her weight. Sap rises through its trunk. It breathes through a thousand singing leaves. It stands, rooted as a living testament to strength.

She asks, "Do you cry when your leaves fall?"

The tree remains, steadfast.

GRIEF

June 18, 2010

2:14p.m.

The man in the moon
is my brother,
face bright yet featureless,
indistinct
and so the face
of every man
who calls out
into the vastness of space
that is not empty
to his mother,
sister, or beloved
child.

If you were to
take flight,
to leave gravity's
insistent tugging
behind
just long enough
to float
on a single breath—

232

if you were to move close
enough to touch
the moon,
then you would know
how time and weather
play here too,
that only from a distance
is this rugged face
radiant
with reflected light.

June 20, 2010

1:17p.m.

The Mother visits the zoo with her Buddhist nun friend. They notice a snow leopard and polar bear caged in the middle of a steaming city afternoon.

These animals look out of place in their artificial habitat that leaves them no room to run.

The Mother feels compassion even for a fearsomely large python who has no space to stretch. His coils are cramped in a vertical glass case.

She returns home, sits at the shrine before an open window, and thinks over the day. Perhaps she feels boxed in by grief, as if she is not free to run or stretch into her full being.

I feel sad without him here.

She could as well say aloud, "I truly loved him. I still love him. This love is truth."

Tears flow like a quiet stream through the hollows of the Mother's face. They run across her cheekbones, into her nostrils, and over her lips and chin.

She tastes salt and grieves not only for the Son but for her grandfather who was burnt to ash.

She grieves for her great-aunt.

To every girl, their mother-figure is indeed the most powerful woman in the world—a role model, comforter, supporter, and protector.

How could she not have been immortal?

The Mother remembers that with her great-aunt's death had also come a new kind of freedom. Gone was the unconscious desire to please her, to live up to who she might have wanted the Mother to be.

The Mother had transformed. A certain intensity had lifted. She had begun to grow into herself, into the woman who she is, today.

What is there is about today that awakens deeper grief? Nothing is wrong with today. There is beauty in the light of today.

Though up until today, the Mother has been busy—busy preparing to launch the next issue of the literary magazine, busy preparing for an upcoming meditation workshop, and busy preparing to submit a new book manuscript.

With preparations completed, there is little to do now.

Today, she has time to feel.

Feelings of grief are normal.

Feelings of sorrow change, like the seasons.

Beyond these windows, the sun rises, the sun sets, and the sun will rise again.

The Mother sits at the altar, with its pictures, flower buds, and candles. She looks up into the face of the open sky.

She receives the blessing of this space and time to pray in the silence.

5:42p.m.

The Mother thinks now of abandoning her work and who she is supposed to be. She considers disappearing from this city and traveling to Africa. There, the natives will take her in with no questions asked and care for her as their very own child. She will disappear from here.

We will each disappear from this material world, one day. We must return to the source of creation.

It is quite normal for the Son to have gone, and for the Mother to yearn for him. This experience is a luminous point of connection between hundreds of millions of lives in the vast universe—grief. So, too, is joy.

The Mother loves the grief, because she loved the Son so.

June 22, 2010

2:35p.m.

The experience is simple.
I am lying on the floor,
gazing at the bamboo tree.
It leans over a small, painted bureau,
the two drawers,
one atop the other,
empty but for bare necessities.
I don't need much these days.

2:46p.m.

Gazing at the bamboo tree,
I remember the young palm
that stood in the corner
of my first place—
on the East side, just
six blocks north
of the 59th Street bridge.
I remember two rooms,
their plaster walls crumbling.
I remember the long air shaft
that carried clear sound—

an opera singer running
up and down the scales,
a woman at the peak of love.

I wanted to be an artist then,
though I contemplated politics.
Somehow, I would change the world.

Today, the most important
element of experience
may simply be this:
I am here.

I am lying on the floor,
gazing at the bamboo tree.
There is light
at the window.

June 26, 2010

4:23 p.m.

The Mother walks almost daily in the park.

She appreciates creation.

Today, a rainbow rises from the reservoir. The rainbow is vibrant. It is larger, brighter, and more colorful than any she has seen, though it is only an illusion.

She walks paths overgrown with flowers to let go of the pain. They bloom untamed.

There is a young patch of black-eyed daisies. These flowers look like the daisies that the Son's nurse brought over, in his memory.

"They're bright, like he is," she said when she gave them to the Mother.

The Mother stops and stands with these flowers for several minutes. They look like him—wide-eyed and perpetually amazed. Somehow, amazed by her.

"I grieve," she tells the open sky.

June 28, 2010

11:07a.m.

The Mother takes a bus upstate. She visits a small temple situated on eighty vast acres of wilderness.

There is no traffic on these paths, no horns honking or exhaling of exhaust.

She stops briefly to let a flock of wild geese pass.

She greets old friends. They are glad to see her. She has not visited in months, since before the Son got sick.

The Mother feels comfortably self-sufficient here.

She curls up in front of the shrine to the Blessed Mother. The incense, offered that morning, is still fragrant. She rests her head gently on a pile of brocaded pillows. Indeed, she is held in the Blessed Mother's lap.

In being nurtured, the Mother is able to piece together the fragments of her life and continue.

June 29, 2010

3:06p.m.

I feel sad here without him.

The Mother says these words aloud, several times. To acknowledge feelings of sorrow is to be relieved of them.

She will not wall up her grief. She will express herself. She can speak, write, dance, or sing the grief. She can make a prayer of this grief. She can release grief, letting it resound and echo into space, into the space of other sentient beings, into the space of life that continues as a divine mystery.

Yes, the Mother feels sad here without the Son.

She knows another truth, too. This truth is that she is still whole, that these feelings will pass, that she holds beautiful memories.

To long for the Son is to continue loving him.

She holds the Son in the heart, even as she can no longer hold him in her arms.

June 30, 2010

11:17a.m.

I would not say that my way
should be your way, for there is
no way.

I will say simply,
go out into an open field
where there may be
lilies or oak trees
or a pond with a worn bridge
of grey slatted wood
and the growth of moss,
ducks and a few passersby,
city kids with cell phones,
a family with two small girls
who speak with British accents,
a man with a camera
who wants so desperately
to keep your beauty
as you stand
amazed in stillness,
and look beyond all this

243

GRIEF

into the sky,
blue
so far
so distant
so endlessly expansive
and so close that
it's touching you now.

July 1, 2010

5:46p.m.

The Mother considers the path before her. The path is not her path. The path is the path.

Sometimes, we stride along briskly, rigorously. Sometimes, we slow down to step carefully through uneven terrain. We continue along the path in accordance with life circumstances and the mind's response.

Even so, the path remains the path. We put one foot in front of the other. We don't bemoan the sharp stones and dry twigs that litter the dirt around our feet. We look up. We look ahead. We focus on the truth before us.

We need not be distracted by loss or sorrow. We need not lose sight of the truth that lights our way. So, we find encouragement and continue.

This truth is within us.

7:12p.m.

In grieving, we can be gentle with ourselves. We need not be overwhelmed.

We stay present with our feelings. The breath consoles us in our pain.

We allow anguish to arise in the context of a greater peace that is like a silent lake, or the endless sky.

We support the mind with structure.

We focus one simple task at a time, finishing one thing before beginning another— slowly, kindly, and deliberately continuing with our lives.

We notice what has been well-done. There is no need to dwell on what has yet to be done. We appreciate simple progress. We expect ourselves to be no different than we are. We allow ourselves the open space to mourn and to heal.

When the mind writhes, disturbed by emotion, we find solace in friendship or take comfort in solitude. We pray all the more in our distress.

How blessed are we to hold such treasures in the heart as friendship, solitude, and prayer.

So, we open into a deeper and more integrated experience—holding the tender infant sorrow, while bathing in the light.

8:49p.m.

The fragrant flower of compassion blooms radiant in the night of despair, and in the morning, there is glory.

Never is experience wasted. Whatsoever we live through fires us, until we are of such purity that the goldsmith is able to make of us the instrument that he wishes us to be.

Rejoice, rejoice, for so we open unto eternity, here on this dusty earth of love and loss, and beyond all beyond into luminous salvation.

July 2, 2010

2:45p.m.

Grief may be a subtle shade of loneliness.

It is certainly love's shadow.

We are used to having someone around, and now he is no longer here. How we thirst. Yes, death feels like the longing of baked and cracking earth, the endlessly hot glass sands that reach for miles with no water in sight, the open salty sea that yearns for the sky with no glimpse of land.

The one we love has gone.

He was our hope and our joy.

He was the very reflection and confirmation of our soul.

Yet must we stand before the mirror of another to realize that we are whole? The form of the one we love is no more than a reminder of the truth that dwells forever in the heart—a truth that is vaster than sand or sea, or even sky. Such is love.

To love is an incredible gift.

With loss, we honor love.

We grieve for the love that we once knew. We pray to live in truth beyond this miraculous display of birth and death, this cosmic play of you and me, to awaken suddenly as one in being with the Spirit.

July 4, 2010

11:09a.m.

The grieving heart wants to mourn, but only for some time, only to the point where the sorrow is sweet.

Then, we return our attention to a deeper peace.

This afternoon, the world is simple. There is sensory experience. There is mental experience. There is awareness of these experiences and a greater clarity beyond these experiences.

We might note the events of our lives with seriousness, though we have only to put a gentle smile on our faces and discover steady joy, peace.

Today is a holiday. Independence Day.

The Mother passes the neighborhood church and returns home by way of the supermarket. She stocks up on tomatoes, mozzarella, and pasta—all good things. Her bags overflow with greens, cucumbers, and carrots, with mangoes, bananas, and cherries.

A broad *terra cotta* pitcher full of fruit sits on the kitchen counter.

She will taste the goodness of ripe fruit.

She will celebrate life and freedom.

After the Mother unpacks the groceries from the brown paper bags, she finds that there is still time to enjoy the afternoon—to read, to walk in the park, to pray, and to listen.

The light is strong.

She sits before the shrine, as the sun settles into the deepening blues of twilight.

THE WISDOM OF GRIEF

We will each experience the loss of someone we love. Loss is a part of our shared human experience. We might approach the resulting grief from the perspective of psychologist, chaplain, philosopher, or seeker.

One of the most well-known Indian teachings on grief appears in the Bhagavad Gita. These words are spoken to the sorrowing disciple Arjuna. Arjuna is a warrior who slumps dejected in his chariot, unable to fight. In the midst of the battlefield, the Lord rouses him from grief with these verses.

> *…The wise do not grieve*
> *for the living or the dead.*   2.11

> *Never have we not existed,*
> *nor shall any cease to be.*   2.12

> *Just as the soul experiences*
> *childhood, youth, and old age*
> *through the changes of the body,*

so the soul's journey continues
when it passes on from the body...   *2.13*

The Lord speaks to Arjuna, and the Lord speaks to us, when we grieve on the battlefield of life. He advises us not to sorrow over the living or the dead.

Usually, we think of grief as relating to someone who has died. In this passage, however, the Lord also exhorts us not to sorrow for the living.

How do we make sense of this teaching?

All too often, we do grieve over the actions of the living. Someone has hurt or disappointed us. Someone has failed to do what we had hoped for. The people in our lives are not acting according to the script we have written. So, we are sorrowful.

To grieve in this way is a waste of our precious breath. Here's why: If we are able to make change, then we can act as a catalyst to transform a challenging situation. We empower ourselves and those around us.

If we cannot make change, then we need not allow the mind to spin like a wheel, scattering our mental energy. We center ourselves, and we accept the situation. We continue on the path as it appears before us.

Whether we act effectively or practice acceptance, we do not sorrow over the actions of the living.

Likewise, we need not be mired in sorrow over the passing on of the dead. Death is an inevitable part of life. This how nature works. In fact, transformation is the miracle of the material world.

A child is born. The child grows strong and matures. In time, the young one becomes a parent or a wise elder, only to pass on, leaving the world a better place for the next generation to come.

What arises will fall away, and what falls away will again arise.

The source of this miraculous creation is itself uncreated. The source from which we are born and to which we each return is a steadily luminous presence. This deeper spiritual truth supports nature's transformations of birth, maturation, aging, and death.

According to our material experience, what is created will again return to its source. Meanwhile, the mystic sees that what is born confused will awaken to limitless glory.

All is as it should be. My circumstance and your circumstance fit together perfectly in the celestial pattern of creation. We have each been born for a reason. We experience particular circumstances for a reason—so that we can awaken in the here and now.

Beyond death lives the awakened soul, merged with the source of being. Glory, glory, hallelujah!

When we are in the throes of mourning, however, such teachings seem esoteric, perplexing, or even painful. With the mind adrift in our oceanic grief, we may feel unable to remain steadfast in the light of truth.

Perhaps, we understand intellectually that no one truly dies. Yes, the soul becomes one with all to live on in each of us.

We may even find relief through prayer and meditation.

Still, we weep over the loss of our loved ones.

When the mind suffers like this, we cannot turn our backs or pretend that grief does not exist. Rather, we engage gently with the sorrow.

None of us are automatons, hard-wired with a perpetual grin painted onto our faces, nor should we aspire to be so. As we love, so we feel loss when someone dies.

The point of the verses from the Bhagavad Gita is not to feel nothing. The point is that we do not lose ourselves in sorrow such that we cannot carry on.

We hold grief tenderly as it arises. We give grief time to express itself. We find support through continued prayer and meditation, and in serving each other.

This wise teaching from the Bhagavad Gita, not to lose ourselves in grief, is akin to the teachings of the prophet Joel in the Bible.

Joel tells us not to rend our robes in sorrow. (Such was the custom of his time.) He tells us to rend our hearts. (Joel 2: 12-13)

Joel reminds us that we need not be outwardly ostentatious in expressing our grief. Instead, we allow the grief to create an inner transformation. Sorrow awakens the tender heart, such that we become more deeply connected and compassionate towards each other.

It is often said that what binds a fool liberates the wise. This is undoubtedly true of our feelings. Emotion may bind or liberate, depending on how it is approached.

When handled with sensitivity, grief can be a stepping stone from sorrow to liberation. As grief arises, we are indeed wise to examine it, to understand it, and so to move through confusion into clarity.

Understand that we experience sorrow on a personal level. When we cry over a loss, we are engaged with the emotion of our particular circumstance. This loved one was a cause of my happiness, we might say.

Now that this cause of joy has disappeared, I feel lonely, frightened, sad, and angry.

At this point, we have a choice. We can get stuck in the tar pit of loss and grief, or we can acknowledge our feelings and continue.

How can we go on? We let the love we feel strengthen us.

Indeed grief is born of love: We do not grieve for what we have not loved. So, we embrace the dialectic of loss and love. To hold both loss and love in the heart, is to awaken.

Consider the distinction between transcendent love and personal love. True love is not a love of conditional romance. It is not a love that fades with the bloom of youth, or a love that depends upon somebody's pleasing us. It is a selfless love and so a love of perfect union.

The enlightened sage experiences the light in all. The light in me is the light in you. As such, we cannot be lost to each other, for I am you and you are me.

Realizing that we are each emanations of an inseparable divinity, we begin to take the creative transformations of the world in stride.

Life continues. Ah, so this is how it is, now.

Folklore tells of a humble sadhu and her gentle acceptance of life's transformations. This devout sadhu lived in a mountain hut just beyond a simple village. The sadhu spent her days doing ordinary things— tending to a vegetable garden, sitting in prayer and meditation, and receiving visitors as they approached for advice.

One day, a village woman climbed the path to the sadhu's hut. She was weeping and wailing, bemoaning her fate. She carried a child in her arms.

She knelt at the sadhu's feet to explain her plight. Her lover had abandoned her, while she was with child. She had no way to care for this child, nor was she able to face the stigma of bearing a child out of wedlock. She felt sure that her family and neighbors would not understand how this had happened.

In her distress, she suddenly laid the child at the feet of the sadhu. Then, she turned, and ran back down the path to the village. She stopped not once to look back.

Soon, she had disappeared.

At the feet of the sadhu lay the child wrapped in swaddling clothes.

The sadhu had lived alone for many years. Needless to say, she had never raised a child. Still, as the child reached out with his tiny hands and began to burble, she took him into her arms.

"Ah," she said. "So this is how it is, now."

In time, the infant grew into a strong toddler and then a carefree child. He mulched the garden and became an adept meditator himself. He called the trees his friends, as well as the animals and the villagers. He felt an equal love for all of creation as an expression of divine glory.

"Ah," said the sadhu. "So this is how it is, now."

Some years later, his mother returned. Keeping this child a secret for so long had been too much for her to bear. She had finally confided in her family. They were unexpectedly overjoyed.

The young mother was deeply relieved. She had now returned to claim her child.

She thanked the sadhu for having cared for him during such important and formative years. She saw that the boy was of good health and strong character, and that he was joyful.

"My child could not have had a better caretaker," said the young woman. "I don't know how to thank you."

So saying, she lifted the boy into her arms and carried him with her back to the village. She stopped not once to look back.

"Ah," said the sadhu. "So this is how it is, now." And she stepped out to weed the garden.

How was this sadhu able to take these changes of circumstance in stride?

When we are fulfilled in truth, the dualities of the world do not shake us, so hard. They do not shake us, for the open mind is awash with light.

We remain comfortably centered throughout the cycles of gain and loss, pleasure and pain, infamy and fame, praise and blame, and even birth and death.

We may even realize that these seeming pairs of opposites are actually alike. We recognize that either end of the pole has the potential to send us sprawling.

Just as being unfairly blamed may arouse the heat of passion, so excessive praise may inflate our sense of self. In neither case are we centered in the truth.

Recognizing the equivalent effects of these apparent opposites liberates us.

We may now choose to let go of both sides, and to continue in an ordinary way. The ordinary soul experiences an unchanging sense of well-being that is undisturbed by the ongoing transformations of creation.

To understand duality in this way does not negate our feelings. Emotion is important. When sorrow, anger, or fear arise, we pay attention. We attend to happiness as well, such that we do not get swept off our feet, infatuated by a dream, or let down when our romance with the world does not last.

We remain centered. We realize that emotion arises in the context of vast, open space, and that it subsides again into a deeper peace.

So, we shine steadily.

At the same time, we recognize that our spiritual life is not meant to be an escape from the sorrows of the world. The true test of our awakening is to remain steadily luminous in this shadowy world of love and loss.

As we realize the light, the next step along the path is to share of this truth with others. We live in service, so that all beings may awaken. This is why we are here.

The way that truth is shared may be different for each of us. We contribute as an integrated part of the whole, wide world, according to how we have been created. Truly, we have been made well and for a genuine purpose.

We express truth through our natural gifts and talents. We offer of ourselves without expectation or limitation. We cannot even hope that what we offer be received with thanks or lead to transformation. We simply continue to radiate the light of unconditional truth.

To live in luminosity, we don't need to try hard. In fact, we can relax, let go, and be free.

We untie the mooring ropes of attachment. We allow the boat to float across the river of sorrows to the other shore, where the sun is rising.

All that is asked of us is that we be who we are.

We can be uncontrived. We connect by letting down the barriers of who we are supposed to be.

We are asked to stand up in bare awareness, showing ourselves to be who we truly are, to be who we have always been, to be one in being with the Spirit.

Truly, this is love.

We experience true love when we are emptied of self.

In transcending the limited personal self, we recognize emotions as different shades of love: Grief is love for what has been lost. Anger is love that has been thwarted. Fear is love of personal self. Happiness is love of temporarily fulfilled desire.

Awakening is love, unbounded. Truth flows freely. The light is boundless. Such is freedom.

May the tears of sorrow wash us clean.

May we live in the truth of infinite love, one in being with the Spirit.

May we be liberated.

HIS LAST WORDS

We have all heard advice on how to grieve:
We give ourselves time.

We acknowledge our feelings, be they anger, fear, loneliness, frustration, or sorrow.

We might expect to plead and to wallow, before finally accepting the void in our lives that our loved once filled. We might try to embrace this hollow loss.

Yes, and we embrace life, too. Rather than being mired in sadness, we try to do what we enjoy. Here we still are, and for this life, we give thanks.

We let our loved one live on in what we have learned and shared, together. It is our duty and our salvation to continue, here, in this world. We are the legacy of love.

We are still here, together.

Sharing of our grief with others, as we would share of our joy and goodness, can bring healing. It is important for families and communities to pull together during times of loss. So, we share the living memories of love.

We allow our loved one to continue to be a vibrant presence, by remembering and talking about him or her. We grieve together, not for days or even weeks, but for as long as it takes. We listen to each other. We comfort each other. We hold each other. We don't pretend that things are "normal" when they are not. We discover that we are not isolated in loss. We attend to each other, we who still live.

We also heal through prayer. We pour our sorrowful hearts out to the Lord.

Each one of us is a beloved child of the Lord. No one is left out, for there is no one whom the Lord's grace cannot touch. Like the rays of the sun, it reaches everywhere, into the darkest corners and crevices of our hearts.

Even as we hide ourselves or deny the truth of love, so love will find us. So, love will renew us. The heart will bloom, again. We need fear no loss, for we are indeed being taken care of.

Love is truly who we are. Love is like the wildflowers that grow free at the edges of meadows, along the dusty, rutted roads, in the crevices of rock and cliff. These untamed flowers need not be delicately tended, though they are tender in their beauty. They bloom spontaneously. Such is the truth of the heart.

In love with life, we appreciate life. We live each moment fully.

We waste no time. Neither do we fear time's passing.

We enjoy ourselves, though we do not squander our breath in idle pleasure.

We find something to be thankful for, each day.

We dare to fulfill our dreams, and then to see beyond them.

In experiencing loss, we grow in compassion for each other. As we move through sorrow, so we wish to alleviate sorrow. Perhaps we express this burgeoning compassion creatively, charitably, or even philosophically. Perhaps we are contemplative, quietly praying for others. Whatever our way may be, we live our lives as a sacred offering for the liberation of all beings.

We trust in the goodness of creation and our place in it. We renew our vows with the absolute truth. We become one with that truth.

We realize—The only truth is love, and love is who we are.

Inspired by the months of cooking and caring for the Son, we founded a women's shelter in New York City. Lalitamba Saranam opened on Easter morning of 2011.

He is risen! May all beings know salvation through the grace and peace of our Lord.

Books by the Author

Mantra and the Goddess
by Swamini Sri Lalitambika Devi
ISBN 978-1-84694-313-3
Mantra Books, 2010

Atma Bodha
by Swamini Sri Lalitambika Devi
ISBN 978-78099-398-0
Mantra Books, 2012

The Lotus Within
by Swamini Sri Lalitambika Devi
ISBN 978-0-9778633-8-9
Chintamani Books, 2012

Mandukya Upanishad
by Varuna
and Swamini Sri Lalitambika Devi
ISBN 978-0-978633-5-8
Chintamani Books, 2013

www.ingramcontent.com/pod-product-compliance
Lightning Source LLC
LaVergne TN
LVHW011219080426
835509LV00005B/214